THE LIVING DESERT

**Written and photographed
by Marycke Jongbloed**

MOTIVATE
PUBLISHING

Published by
Motivate Publishing

PO Box 2331
Dubai, UAE
Tel: (04) 824060
Fax: (04) 824436

PO Box 43072
Abu Dhabi, UAE
Tel: (02) 311666
Fax: (02) 311888

London House
26/40 Kensington High Street
London W8 4PF
Tel: (071) 938 2222
Fax: (071) 937 7293

Directors:
Obaid Humaid Al Tayer
Ian Fairservice

First published 1987
Reprinted 1988
Third printing 1993

© **Motivate Publishing 1987**

ISBN 1 873544 02 2

Printed by Emirates Printing Press, Dubai

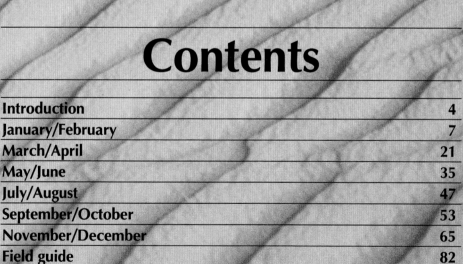

Contents

Cover photographs: The white flowers of Eremobium aegyptiacum – literally "desert life" – dot the sands. Inset: Beetle investigates a yellow Tribulus flower; dew glistens on Silene villosa. Back cover inset: Moringa oleifera hosts a hungry visitor.

INTRODUCTION

When I arrived in the United Arab Emirates in May 1983, I knew very little about the desert. Coming from the wet, green Dutch countryside I was fascinated by the bleakness of the wilderness here, but I expected that the novelty would soon wear off and I had brought a number of medical courses and study-books to keep myself occupied in what I expected to be a mainly indoor life.

How different it turned out! The very first lecture at the UAE Natural History Group Al Ain branch that I attended was about the wild flowers of this area. I had not noticed any, and I assumed that the speaker, from the Abu Dhabi group, must be an expert to know so much.

Even though I started to explore my surroundings that autumn, it was not till the following spring that I discovered the desert flowers. I found hardly any guides or reference books to help me identify what I found. Fortunately the flower expert from Abu Dhabi, Rob Western, was very helpful and started me on the road to recording desert flora. (He, by the way, turned out to be as much of an amateur as I was, and had learned all his botany in a mere three years).

When you look at flowers, you cannot help but see insects and small reptiles too. Again, only rarely could a book be found as a reference, and, in general, the prices of these coffee-table editions were prohibitive. It was good fortune once more to meet an expert - a true one this time. Claus Curt Mueller (CC), my partner on the desert walks described in this book, is a walking encyclopedia, knowing not only names, but more importantly, functions and ecological relations. He taught me to observe and made me aware of the threats that exist for the delicate wildlife of this area. I learned about animals that had lived here once and have disappeared; about those whose existence is threatened by extinction now; and about what will happen to the desert if we do not take care of it.

Writing about what I saw in the desert was never part of my plan. It started quite accidentally, when a whale washed up on the shore of Jebel Dhanna. Waleed Al Tikriti, of the Department of Antiquities, wanted to collect the bones to save them for a future Natural History Museum. I went along when he made the trip north, and was present when he found that a large number of important bones had gone missing. We tried to think of a way to find these bones, and I offered to write an article in the newspaper, illustrated by a drawing of the missing parts. The small article, duly printed by the Khaleej Times, had immediate success: within a week the missing bones had been returned by members of the Abu Dhabi Natural History Group, who had picked them up some time before. The Khaleej Times meanwhile asked me to continue to write for the paper.

Those observations and drawings of plants and insects have grown into this book, presented as a guide to a typical year. If it helps fellow enthusiasts to take an interest in the world around them, then it has served its purpose. It takes only a pair of feet, careful eyes and a curious mind, and the beauty of the living desert can be yours.

A WHALE OF A PROBLEM

By Marycke Jongbloed

"**I**n the middle of April, a small plane was landing on the airstrip near Jebel Dhanna. As he was coming down, the pilot saw something floating in the water near the coast. It looked like an upturned boat with men clinging onto the hull.

As soon as he landed, the pilot notified the authorities. A rescue team went out. However, to their surprise they found not a wrecked boat, but a whale being devoured by sharks. A rare find in Gulf waters. The whale was not identified at the time, but its skeleton washed up on the beach near the Golf Club area.

Someone told the archaeologist of the Al Ain Museum, Dr Walid Al Tikriti, about the episode in June. He expressed keen interest, because the museum is making plans to develop a Natural History collection, and the whale would be a great addition to the dugong skeleton that he already had.

He rushed to the spot to investigate and, to his delight, the skeleton was quite complete. the nine-foot-long lower jaw-bones (if that was what they were) were especially impressive. He arranged with the local authorities to collect the skeleton after Ramadan. Since it lay in an area of the beach that is restricted to the public, he did not think it necessary to hide or guard the bones.

Unfortunately, that turned out to be a mistake. Early this month, a small expedition went down to collect the skeleton. When Dr Al Tikriti arrived at the scene, it turned out that several of the bones were missing: the two magnificent jaw-bones; a whole section of what looked like the cervical vertebrae, seven in all; and another six to eight vertebrae from another part of the spine.

This is really quite a disaster, for it is a difficult job to reconstruct an animal like this, but if parts are missing it is almost impossible. Even if one of the jawbones was still there, the other one could be copied, but now all we have is a picture that shows only part of one. We do have a picture of the section of cervical certebrae (see drawing), but even from that it would be hard to judge the actual size and shape of the missing bones. It would be so much better to have the real thing!

Needless to say, the museum and the Emirates Natural History Group would be delighted to retrieve some or all of the missing pieces. We have posted a notice at the Golf Club and we hope that it-and this article-may bring some results. As we said in the notice: future generations will be grateful- and so will we! "

(Reprinted from the Khaleej Times, July 24, 1984).

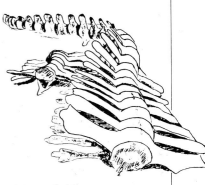

Whale skeleton on the beach of Jebel Dhana.

Chapter 1

JANUARY
FEBRUARY

Spring comes early in the Gulf, and, just as in northern countries, it is heralded by hyacinths. When I see the delicately pink-tinged buds of the desert hyacinths emerging from the sand, I know the season of the desert flowers has started. A few busy months follow: there is much plant-collecting to be done, pressing and mounting of specimens for the Herbarium of the Emirates Natural History Group.

The light in the early hours of the morning is best for photography. After the night fogs have cleared, the days can be crystal clear, with all the dust having been cleaned out of the air.

This is the time to be out and about. The daily temperatures range from 10 to 17 °C and, even if the humidity is high at times, you do not notice it. Desert hikes are easy, for you do not need to carry extra water, and you can go for hours without becoming exhausted.

In a lucky year, there will be rain during these months - showers or even prolonged rainfall. Should you go camping, never pitch tents in a wadi, for flash floods are not uncommon and can be very dangerous. If you camp in the mountains, precautions against malaria are necessary.

Parasitic plants

At the foot of Jebel Hafeet are some low dunes with a lot of vegetation which lead up to the huge bare sand dunes of the Empty Quarter. The area is bordered by mesquites and dotted with tamarix trees, large zygophyllum bushes and clumps of *Hammada elegans* in various stages of fruiting. A few palm trees are witness to man's attempt to cultivate the area.

I started walking, and within the first few metres spotted something that delighted me: several strange, dark red growths emerging from the sands, which I recognized as *Cynomorium coccineum* or red thumb. Until then I had only once found one and that was in Dubai. That one was old and had finished flowering. These were in several stages of development. Some bedu had been there before me, judging from the footprints, and the number of plants that had been dug out. Red thumbs are a favourite gourmet food. The young shoots must resemble asparagus. Many medicinal properties are ascribed to these odd mushroom-like plants. I quote from *Medicinal Plants of North Africa* by Loutfy Boulos, published in 1983: "Entire plant aphrodisiac, spermatopoietic, tonic, astringent. Dried plant powdered and mixed with butter used for biliary obstruction. Powder added to meat dishes as a condiment."

Some plants were still intact. Two young shoots coming up through the sand had caused a minute sandslide. They looked like pink thumbs with the skin cobble-stoned with triangular darker patches. An older flowering thumb stood nearby. The flowers consisted of tiny hairs emerging from the velvety covering of the upper end of the plant. It is attractive to flies and I thought it might smell bad but when I sniffed it, did not find that the case.

As I walked around I saw many patches where these strange Maltese mushrooms, as they are also called, had been, the long, dark brown and black stalks taking on bizarre shapes as the plant died. Since they have no chlorophyll of their own, they must use that of other plants. When the seeds fall in the neighbourhood of, for instance, a zygophyllum plant, they send out filaments that attach to the roots of the host plant and in that way they obtain whatever they need to grow - true parasites.

Cynomorium coccineum is a parasitic plant living off the roots of nearby host plants.

On salty soil one can find two parasitic plants: the red thumb and the desert hyacinth.

Close-up of a desert hyacinth.

The one other parasitic plant of the desert, the desert hyacinth or *Cistanche tubulosa,* was also prevalent in this area. It is much more spectacular than the red thumb, consisting of a stalk of large yellow flowers, later turning to soft purple shades, emerging straight from the sand. They like some moisture, which is why they can be found, for instance, on the sprinkler-irrigated road-dividers of the Abu Dhabi-Al Ain road, where they live as parasites of the oleander bushes.

Lunch hour in the desert

On a winter afternoon, I ventured into an irrigated area to see whether the cooler weather had prompted the plants to flower.

The first flowers that I encountered were those of the *Aerva javanica* or ra' bushes, shrubs with tiny white flowers close to the stems. The very fluffy seeds are used for stuffing camel seats and pillows. Similar flowers and seeds grow on the *Cornulaca leucacantha* shrub, but since the stems are studded with very tough, sharp thorns, it would not be easy to gather the fluff.

Ochradenus baccatus attracts many insects.

Another large bush that is currently in flower is the *Hammada elegans*. Large clumps are visible everywhere and, especially when the light is behind the bushes, the subtle white, pink or purple colours of the paper-thin petals are beautiful to see. Those silvery petals are actually fruit wings, which can be blown about by the wind and so carry the seeds. The spiky bushes of *Ochradenus baccatus* or 'kurd' are just starting to show their yellow flowers, while some still carry the clusters of large white berries of last year. As soon as the flowers open, the bush will attract a large number of insects - a nice subject for study for the interested entomologist.

I had set out to photograph a number of grasses. As I sat down to take a shot of a clump of sedge, I saw a small movement near my elbow - a green stem had moved. I looked closer and saw a bright orange eye staring at me. A five inch grasshopper sat hidden among some stems, looking exactly like its surroundings. The bright green insect had straw-coloured ends to its body, legs and antennae, just like a leaf that had begun to wither in the heat of the sun. The creature sat obligingly still, so I could photograph it in several poses, but when I tried to catch it, it flew away. I followed it for several jumps, but finally lost it

The paper thin fruit-wings of Hammada elegans.

The Towerhead grasshopper is a master of camouflage.

thanks to its magnificent camouflage. I have seen this Towerhead Grasshopper also in an all-over sandy colour, sitting on some sandy-coloured rocks, and now I am wondering whether it has chameleon-like properties?

Several small geckos and dozens of red and white dotted butterflies were too swift to be captured on film, but chasing them around, I came upon a number of interesting plants: Many new seedlings of the Arabian Primrose or al hammar, the roots of which are used for rouge; the indigo plant with its tiny red flowers and hundreds of miniature seed pods; clusters of yellow launea around a sprinkler head; and one flowering *Taverneara aegyptiaca.* Last

Seedlings of the Arabian primrose Arnebia hispidissima.

The Toadheaded agama lives among the bushes on the gravel plain.

year I had only found branches with the orchid-like fruit-wings, but now the bright purple flowers were in evidence. (See S10).

Most of the fifteen different species of weeds which I saw have flowers no larger than a few millimetres in diameter, but the shapes and colours are wonderful and well worth a close look.

And a one-hour lunch break is all it takes to enjoy it!

Qatar foothills

I turned off the road to Mahdah to follow a track which I thought would lead to the base of Jebel Qatar. When we had used it a few months earlier, it was rough but passable. This time, however, I lost the track after only a mile or so, and noticed that the sand was deeper than I remembered. By the time I realised that I had taken the wrong turning, and decided to go back it was too late. The car was stuck in the sand up to the hubs.

There I was, typical novice, stuck without a spade, without extra water, on an early Friday morning. However, it was not the deep desert and it was still cool. I was only a short distance from the main road and, as it turned out, the area was a favourite weekend haunt for local families.

The first driver, a father with kids, who stopped to help had a lot of sympathy but no shovel. The second car that stopped disgorged a group of young adults who tackled the problem with gusto, but no amount of shovelling had any effect - a tow rope was needed. Some of the guys drove off to get one while others stayed with me. One of them held a small reptile. I asked what it was and they explained that it lived in the sand and made a delicious snack. The purpose of their outing was to catch these creatures for a gourmet picnic lunch!

It was a beautifully-marked animal, sand coloured with a dark brown pattern on its back. Its skin had a glossy sheen like glazed porcelain. Its jaws were shaped like those of a miniature alligator, and to judge from the way in which its captor gingerly held the animal, they could probably inflict a painful bite. The stubby legs had feet with fringed toes. Later I found out that this was a skink, also called a Sand fish, since it can swim through loose sand like a fish swims through water.

Its streamlined, smooth body and fringed toes are

great assets for this activity. Once, we released such a sand fish and watched it. It made a rapid movement with its tail and hind legs and sank into the sand within a split second without leaving a trace. We dug it up immediately and watched its lightning disappearance again - but when we waited for a few seconds after that, it was nowhere to be found. Under the surface of the sand it had moved away, without our seeing where it went, even though we were watching closely.

The boys came back with a piece of steel wire and pulled the car loose. They invited me to breakfast with their families and, with one of the desert veterans behind the wheel, we drove at breakneck speed through the bushes across the plain to a dry wadi. There, in the shade of two giant ghaf trees, a large group of adults and children were frolicking in the mild morning sunshine. I joined them for a morning of friendly talk and local meals (though I cleverly avoided the skink snack!)

Assubaithi

The road in front of us dipped down steeply to the bottom of a wadi. The scenery was spectacular: several canyons converging upon the main wadi had carved out towering islands of layered sediment rock. Except for some dried up pulicaria and fagonia plants, there was nothing to see but stone — grey, brown, ochre, orange and sepia-coloured rocks. We eased the car across the bumpy wadi bed and climbed out on the other bank.

Here more plants were apparent: euphorbia, zygophyllum and a yellow flowered plant which I had never seen before. A mile or so further on we could see terraced fields and a palm grove with a small house at the roadside where a dog and a donkey were standing guard.

The wadi had to be traversed again, and then the road ended. At this point a dam had been built, but there was no water to form the lake that should have been there. At the bottom of this would-be reservoir a veritable garden grew. I was quite excited at finding several species that I had not seen before. Some I knew from pictures like the *Cleome glaucescens*, whose Arabic name is 'muqaybil ash shams' or sun-facer because its petals are always turned towards the sun. Others were not described in any of the books I had access to: a recumbant pink pea, a

The skin of the Sand fish looks like glossy porcelain.

A courtyard with some large pottery jars.

The little pink peaflower of Argyrolobum roseum.

huge thistle, and an odd little plant with tiny white flowers resting on fruit-wings that were velvety, bright pink, and studded with silvery hairs. In the one location there were single specimens of a dozen different species of plants. A large specimen of *Physorrhyncus chaemarapistum* had a pretty butterfly fluttering around its mauve flowers. This plant always attracts a lot of insects, as do the thistles.

We climbed up the path towards the oasis - one of the best kept places I had ever seen. The scent of flowering citrus was heavy on the air. The path was so steep that, at one point, my eyes were level with the next terrace, and at such close proximity I could not miss the beautiful small flowers that were growing between the grasses: *Anagallis arvensis,* locally called camel's eyes or 'ayn al jamal'.

It is a blue version of the European scarlet pimpernel, and one of the loveliest flowers I know. It has deep cornflower blue petals with a dark red base surrounding a crown of golden stamens and a white pistil - all of this only about five mm in diameter. The little meadow was lovely, with yellow daisies vying for attention with the blue camel's eyes in the shade of the date palms and the lemon trees.

To the right, small plots were separated by cemented watercourses. We heard the rush of water and saw a farmer bent over a falaj arranging rocks to divert the stream. We called out a greeting and he came towards us, his face all crinkled up in smiles: "Yes, you are welcome to see the nakheel. Salaam, salaamkum".

The view on the left was in stark contrast with the lush greenery on the right. A wide wadi, dozens of metres below, separated us from the bleak hills on the far side, where the mountains rose up to towering heights. Several rugged valleys opened up into the main wadi, and a sparse growth of trees at various spots indicated the presence of water.

CC scanned the hillsides with his binoculars, as always intent on catching a glimpse of the Arabian tahr. This is a species of mountain goat, which has become very rare - indeed it is almost extinct. It is extremely shy and avoids human contact, but it needs daily access to water. Therefore, isolated wadis like these are the most likely places to find one. But it is quite a few years since the last positive sighting of one was reported.

The path led us deeper into the oasis, where a few houses were grouped together. In a courtyard a few large pottery jars lay in a corner.

Just below the houses another dam had been built to form a small pond from which the irrigation of the oasis could be controlled. The falaj that led into this pond followed the contours of the hillside for a mile or more. A narrow track ran beside it, offering a magnificent view of the canyon below. We followed it until it was time to turn back in the failing light.

Extinction is forever

I had been told about wild orchids growing in a certain wadi and flowering sometime in January. Every three weeks or so I had made a quick trip to the site to check on them. The first time only old withered stalks pinpointed the exact site where they would be. Later, fresh green shoots appeared, but so far I had not seen any buds or flowers. This time I was sure I would be lucky....

We walked through the oasis, admiring the huge mango trees and the ripening oranges. The bulbuls twittered high overhead and the toads had multiplied with the advent of cooler weather and a more abundant water supply. We reached the spot where a dense palm grove straddled the low-lying stream and a small pond. I spotted an orchid plant - and immediately cried out in alarm: "It's been cut! Somebody was here earlier and took the flowers!" We searched around frantically, but everywhere the adult plants had been decapitated with a knife or scissors. Whoever took the flowers had been so thorough that not even a bud remained.

As there were no flowers left on these plants there would be no pollination and no seeds. Cutting off all the flowers of all the specimens of one plant is the fastest and surest way to bring about extinction of that species. If it is a rare plant, that may mean that no one on earth will see that particular flower again - ever!

I was quite upset, thinking that this would put an end to orchids in this particular location. I wished people would be more considerate of the treasures of nature, especially in an arid environment where the balance between all living things is so delicate. If we venture out we should just look, never disturb.

It is far more difficult to photograph or sketch a flower than to pick it - but the end result can be enjoyed far longer, and the original can be enjoyed by other people after us, into future generations! If an insect is picked up to be studied, it should be

No picture of the Arabian tahr can be taken in the wild, as the animal has become extinct in the UAE.

Epipactis veratrifolia is the only species of orchid in the wadis.

The seed pods of Ephedra foliata.

returned to its habitat afterwards even if it means going a long way back to where it was found. Driving with four-wheel-drive vehicles in the desert should be done carefully, always sticking to established tracks where possible. It is so easy to drive across a rare plant, or to destroy the burrow of a reptile or a rodent without even noticing it. Even "duning" in the ostensibly bare sands with dune buggies destroys fragile plant and animal life that is just barely "hanging in" there. Roughing it is a lot of fun, but we need to realise that extinction is forever!

Fortunately, in this case, we did find the orchids in another location. We crossed a shallow stream and found a small pond, reflecting palm trees and sparkling sunlight. It was bordered by luxuriant ferns, and between these were dozens of orchids, most of them still in bud, but some flowering. The greenish yellow and maroon petals curved gracefully back from the bulging lower lip. There were about 12 flowers to each stem, but only one or two were completely open at one time. There were so many here that I had a hard time finding a spot to crouch to take photographs without trampling a plant. But even this tranquil place of beauty was vulnerable, as it turned out a year later when I revisited it: the pond had been deepened, and three feet of mud had been dumped right on top of the orchid plants which had been unable to penetrate it - and so had died a sticky death!

A dried-up puddle

In a deep hollow between two hills a pool of rain water had apparently collected, which had since dried up. The thorough soaking of the soil had coaxed dormant seeds lying there to sprout, and a variety of annuals were present. One conspicuous blue flower was new to me: the flower resembled a gentian, while the leaves were a bit sticky and had a strong herbal smell. (See G 33). Another "unknown" was a small, ground covering plant with squarish seed pods which were dark brown and ribbed.

It was later identified as *Corchorus olitorius*, the jute plant. It is often encountered in plantations where it can grow quite large and looks less stunted than it did here. Closely related is the prostrate *Corchorus depressus* which indeed looks a bit as if someone had sat down on it. It lies so close to the ground that neither leaves nor flowers are taller than two or three millimetres.

The strangest plant here was a leafless vine which grew in a tangle on top of some other plants. The stems branched at right angles and ended in a bunch of greenish capsules which were partially split open to reveal a reddish seed. This turned out to be *Ephedra foliata,* a vine which needs another tree or shrub to cling to. I found them several times on ghaf trees.

A bit further along the path was a specimen of what I call the popcorn plant, first seen in Assubaithi. I now knew that its name was *Pseudogaillonia hymenostephana* and that the velvety cushion from which the tiny, trumpet-shaped flower emerges is, in fact, the calyx. When the flower dies off the calyx becomes lighter in colour and bloated, stretching until it is papery thin and white like popcorn. This light contraption holds the seeds, which can be carried away as if by private balloon to far off places to establish a new plant.

Khutwa

For once we had a four-wheel-drive vehicle at our disposal and we set out on a track that I had been eyeing longingly for quite a while. We traversed a flat plain where the only sign of life was a kestrel falcon which hovered and swooped down towards the rocky ground. We wondered what he could possibly find to eat in that wasteland, and wished him luck...

The road became rougher and the mountains loomed closer. A white mosque seemed lost between the stark hills, but, when we rounded a corner of the track, we saw the new village of Khutwa gleaming in the midday sun.

We passed it and drove on, not knowing where the road would lead us. Then we reached the top of a hill and I could not keep myself from gasping with delight. A huge oasis lay in front of us. The green of the palm trees, the brown hills and the blue and white sky were a pleasing harmony of colours. We drove down towards it and were soon shut in by dense groves on either side of the wall-lined lane. We found a place to leave the car and started walking. The cool wind rustled the greenery, water gurgled nearby and bursts of bird-song reverberated between the tops of trees and hills. To our left we

The purplish arrow of Achyranthes aspera.

Enormous boulders in the gorge of the wadi.

heard children laughing, and further away, to our right, a man was singing as he worked. Guided by the sound of running water, we made our way along the cultivated patches of soil beneath the trees. The water in the falaj, when we reached it, was deep and swift and its passage made the maidenhair ferns tremble. A nice specimen of the everlasting *Gnaphalium luteo-album* drew our attention.

As we positioned ourselves to photograph it, we saw a large funnel web stretched out across the face of a low stone wall. Deep inside the centre hole I could see the creator of this clever construction. The web was like a tissue cone of 30cm diameter. Any insect landing on it would make its way "downhill" to its inevitable death at the bottom of the cone. As I sat quietly beside the web, the spider emerged gingerly, ready to dart back in a split second.

The oasis was full of flowering weeds: the yellow star of *Oxalis corniculata,* the small buttercup of *Sida urens,* the purplish arrow of *Achyranthes aspera* and the bright red berries of *Withania somnifera.*

When we reached the wadi at the far side of the palm groves, we could hear the water rushing in the gorge from afar. Some gorge! I tried to peer down into the chasm, but had to sit down to combat vertigo. The water was some 60 feet below us, and aeons of eroding water had cut fantastic shapes into the rocks: whirlpools with smooth, round sides, razor-sharp wedges and round arches.

Upstream, a rockfall had tumbled huge boulders into the canyon. Downstream, the wadi was wide and flanked by large oases. Across the narrow gorge at our feet lay a bridge made out of four separate palm tree trunks. It looked too flimsy to me to attempt a crossing, even if I had not been afraid of heights. A long way down, on a shelf protruding from the sheer cliff, lay the carcass of a donkey that had missed its footing.

We walked downstream to where the palm groves skirted the wadi edge, looking across some rock pools towards the oasis that clung to the precipitous mountain slope on the other side. Then we scrambled, like mountain goats, along the steep hill to reach a small terraced field on top.

From a distance these small fields looked brown, dry and barren. But, now that we actually stood on one, it turned out to be a little meadow of wild flowers. There were several types of grasses, from the tall juicy napier grass, to the dry plumes of 'khazam-zam' *(Chloris virgata)* and the four-pointed stars of

Dactyloctenium aegyptium. Close to the edge the bright blue pimpernel predominated. The flowers were a very deep blue colour here and I sat down for a close-up of a particularly spectacular one. And, as so often happens, once you slow down, sit and look around, other things come into focus which could have been passed by very easily.

A group of tiny lilies caught my eye. I recognized them immediately as *Asphodelus fistulosus,* having seen them in books before. It was much smaller than I expected (later I saw much larger specimens). The graceful white bells, striped with maroon, were no larger than six mm across with several flowers to each stem. The leaves resembled those of chives and later I found out that chives belong to the lily family also. A few feet away grew another new find: a pale yellow snapdragon of approximately the same size. The flowers were so small and fragile that it seemed impossible that they could grow in such a stark, awe-inspiring environment of bleak mountains and wide wadis. The wadi at this point divided into the narrow gorge at our feet and a wider arm. The two merged again half a mile downstream. A local farmer told us that when the rains come, not only does the gorge fill to the brim, but the water overflows onto the island. That would give credence to the story I had heard that this island, which looked as bleak as the moon, is alive with butterflies after a good rainfall. If this little meadow in which we stood was anything to go by, the island must be covered with wild flowers, if it ever became soaked long enough for the dormant seeds to start growing!

In the afternoon the petals of Silene villosa curl up (see also C 31)

Mushref park

I have discovered a wonderful place right on my doorstep: The Mushref National Park.

I visited it one morning late in January. Immediately after entering the wooded hills, I saw an unusual sight: beneath the ghaf tree and the desert thorns the ground was covered in yellow. Thousands of yellow daisies made this part of the park look like the well remembered spring meadows of Europe. It was a joy to walk around here. Swift little sun-birds, now in their iridescent dark plumage, flitted across the field. Bulbuls warbled in the higher trees. Two squat partridges trundled sedately across the path. I had never seen them from such a short distance, for

A closely grazed bush of Lycium shawii, the desert thorn.

usually they take flight noisily when anyone approaches.

An 'arta' bush was beautifully decorated with bright red tufted lampions. I love the delicate flower of this *Calligonum comosum:* rounded white petals and a circle of bright red stamens. It is very small, but since it occurs at the same time as the lampion seed pods, a flowering bush can hardly be missed.

Several small legumes were hidden between large groups of goosefoot seedlings. One with yellow pea-flowers had very unusual seed pods. They were semi-circular with square notches on their long side. Later I found it is called *Hippocrepis bicontorta.*

Another small legume had a relatively large cyclamen-coloured flower, three grouped together at the top of the plant. A very lovely plant, of which I saw only one specimen. I saw the small *Silene villosa* plants everywhere, but the flowers were already curled up. I have always found them like this - it needs an early morning trip to find them opened up.

Outside the park fence a herd of goats was giving

Mushref Park in spring: a carpet of yellow daisies.

short shrift to a field of eremobium plants. The habitat on both sides of the fence is identical, but inside, the trees have grown to nice shapes and good size, with branches trailing low, and the ground is covered with many pretty ephemerals. Outside only barren sand stretches between stunted stumps and trees grazed to camel height. What a sight this desert could be but for the voracious appetites of goats and camels!

After the rains

Someone had told me that there was a field of lilies at the foot of Fossil Rock near the village of Milaiha. The road south from Dhaid led through green pastures. The rains that had inundated the plains had started the seeds growing much earlier than usual.

The interesting fact about desert annuals is that a small shower will not result in a lot of greenery. The seeds have a protective covering that will not dissolve in just a little bit of water. They have to soak for several days before they will germinate. Where puddles collect in low lying areas you will find new plants even in years with little rain, while the surrounding desert stays bare. Yet all that desert soil is full of seeds that are only waiting for a really good downpour.

The most common plant along the roadside was *Cleome aff. glaucescens,* a very verdant plant with inconspicuous orange flowers and large pea-pods. Where one species grows in profusion there will be others, so we stopped the car and started walking. Between the cleome plants, lots of small stuff was indeed growing. There was the little geranium with its characteristic Stork's bill seed pods. When the seeds are ripe, the pod breaks open at the lower end and the seeds emerge, attached by a white, feathery hair to the still-closed upper end of the pod. The three seeds per pod will flutter in the wind like silvery weather vanes until they are finally carried away. Even as they are fluttering in the breeze you can see tiny corkscrew structures attached to the seeds. When the seed lands on soil, this structure turns out to be useful: in a dry environment it will stay immobile, but if the soil is moist the corkscrew will bore itself into the ground, thus anchoring the seed. The mechanism is hygroscopic, a mechanism employed in various ways by a number of desert plants. (I read somewhere that this particular little

A field of Asphodelus lilies.

The seeds of Erodium sp. are attached to feathery hairs.

corkscrew hair is so sensitive that it is used by scientists in instruments that measure humidity.)

A second pink flower, this time of the legume family, also had interesting seed pods: they were curved into semi-circles, always in pairs. Close by a bright blue forget-me-not flower was hidden between dark-green leaves that were fortified by stiff hairs. Between these hairs, moisture remains, thus preventing the plant from drying out while their silver colour reflects the sunlight away from the vulnerable leaves.

Locusts are favourite items on the menu of the Bee-eaters.

The Little Green Bee-eater uses burrows in mud-banks as a nesting site.

Animal life was sparse on this plain, in spite of all the vegetation. A butterfly hovered around a *Rhazya stricta* bush, no doubt tempted by the sweet smell of the pale blue flowers.

On a mound of sand covering the roots of a hammada bush two black beetles were fighting for possession of the site. They were Sunflower seed beetles, so named by us because of their appearance. The battle lasted for quite a few minutes, but in the end, one beetle scurried away into the open. As it is dangerous for an insect to be on an open patch of ground, the little creature was frantically casting about for a hiding place. Luckily there were lots of hammada bushes in the neighbourhood providing a maze of roots and branches, in addition to several burrows of different sizes. Soon it reached the shelter of another bush and it calmed down considerably, moving slowly as it reconnoitred its new home. The victor beetle in the meantime was ambling from plant to plant, foraging.

A field of lilies was our next stop. It was not hard to find. Between a plantation and a desert village, at the foot of the saddle between a mountain and a sand dune, the desert was completely green. The asphodelus lilies stood knee-high and everywhere the fragile white bells caught the sunlight. Huge Sodom's apple trees dotted the plain. One had a trunk a foot or more in diameter. I had never seen a specimen quite as large. How old it must be! On several bushes we saw groups of Stainer bugs, the colourful small beetles that can be such a pest to crops. Around one bush buzzed a couple of wasps of the brightest red you can imagine. In *Wildlife of Arabia* is a picture of a Gold Wasp which has that colour. Everywhere grasshoppers could be heard making their loud rattling noise as they moved around. Undoubtedly all these insects were the reason that quite a few birds were present in the trees and on the electricity wires. Three medium-sized birds were frolicking in the air above the field. From their flight pattern it was easy to recognise them as Bee-eaters.

Using the car as a hide, we slowly drove up to a bush in which they perched at times. The binoculars brought them up close, emerald green wings, brown feathers on the head, a bright turquoise face with a bold black stripe through the eye. The sunlight made their feathers glow like a jewel. These were the Little Green Bee-eaters, the species that lives here all year round.

Chapter 2

MARCH
APRIL

A blue carpet of Anagallis arvensis.

It is getting warmer now, with temperatures going up to 35°C and many of the plants have been waiting for these higher temperatures to explode into flower and fruit. The seedlings of the annuals that sprouted in the winter rain will now have grown into good-sized plants, and many will have formed seed pods of all shapes and sizes. The wadis have as much water as they will ever have, and hiking around makes one hot enough to enjoy a refreshing dip (after making sure that doing so would not contaminate the drinking water of a local settlement).

Come along on a few hikes to see what lies out there waiting to be discovered and admired.

Spring in the wadis

A gale force wind swept up the sand of the dunes, so that Jebel Qatar was veiled in dust, but further down the road to Mahdah the air cleared and the sky became visible.

The plain, which is usually studded with dead-looking shrubs, looked quite different today. Little patches of green showed in hollows and ditches, and the "dead" bushes seemed fuller and less grey.

A few yards to the left of the road I saw some bright yellow dots bobbing up and down in the wind. I had never seen flowers there before, so we stopped the car and walked across the rocky ground to a little gully. Dozens of lemon yellow crucifers danced on slender stems that rose up from a rosette of leaves

In spring the yellow cushions of Zygophyllum simplex are everywhere.

A lemon yellow crucifer: Diplotaxis harra.

Erucaria hispanica has a lovely fragrance.

close to the ground. From a description I had read I deduced that these might be *Diplotaxis harra,* a spring ephemeral.

Quite a few less conspicuous flowers were present on this site. I recognised seedlings of *Aizoon canariense.* This is a prostrate, ground-covering plant with succulent leaves which grows in a characteristic star shape. The flowers and fruits are yellowish green and hardly noticeable. Near a larger shrub with tiny yellow inflorescences we found a group of tiny blue flowers which looked like forget-me-nots. One delicate, pink-flowered miniature plant, a member of the Geranium family, reminded me of a Stork's bill.

I went across to one of the ubiquitous greyish bushes and found to my surprise that its branches were covered with tiny oval leaves and woolly white buds from which an exquisite white trumpet-shaped flower emerged. (See G 17).

The bush was so full of buds and flowers that it looked as if it were made of "angel-hair", the glass fibre that we used to decorate the Christmas tree with. The little flowers were lovely, but their scent was incredible. Incredibly awful, that is! They smelled like ripe garbage, and since the plain was covered with these shrubs, all in full flower, we were rather grateful for the strong wind.

Another woolly-looking shrub was blue-tinged and turned out to be *Salvia macilanta,* which looks a little like lavender, but has no scent.

We proceeded towards a distant valley. When we entered it, we found that we had to ford a wadi in several places. The lower fields of a plantation were not under cultivation, but the recent rains had coaxed all manner of wild flowers out of the rocky ground. We walked from plant to plant, delighted with each new find.

Everywhere were the yellow cushions of *Zygophyllum simplex.*

This is a low saltbush with succulent leaves that are almost globular with the moisture they contain. The flowers have five petals, that are placed wide apart, giving it a disjointed look. Between these ground-coverers the taller crucifers provided a second layer of blossoms: the yellow *Diplotaxis,* which we had seen earlier, and a mauve-coloured bloom with fern-like leaves called *Erucaria hispanica.* The small seed pyramids of *Rumex vesicarius,* the local sorrel stood out bright red. I had never seen this plant in flower or seed here yet, and now that I finally came across it, I was surprised at its small size. In years when rain falls copiously, it probably grows taller, but now very few were higher than 10 centimetres. The flowers are very unpretentious, little greenish bells close to the stem. But the trilobate seed pods grow to a large size, and are brilliant red.

The other red-flowering plant was much less obvious: the tiny crimson, flower heads of *Boerhavia diffusa* can easily be missed among the multi-coloured rocks.

Beneath a low tree was a large patch of green that looked unusual. When I came closer the green carpet looked curly, because the feathered leaves were all curved backwards. Pink pea-flowers and curved seed pods hid between the leaves. Even though I took pictures, I forgot to take a specimen, and to this day the plant has not been positively identified, other than as a member of the *Astragalus* family.

A pile of loose rocks was crowned with a large stand of *Forsskahlea tenacissima,* the local non-stinging nettle with its red stems and serrated hairy leaves. We always call it the velcro plant, because the leaves and twigs will cling to your clothes.

The flowers of Rumex vesicarius are very unpretentious.

Along the rapidly flowing falaj all sorts of grasses and weeds were growing in profusion. The pink flowers of *Centaurium pulchellum* stood over two feet high, already tightly closed in the relative gloom of the oasis. Where dense stands of maiden hair ferns almost obliterated the falaj, we found orchids: *Epipactis veratrifolia.*

The sprays of green and maroon flowers were nicely camouflaged in the sun speckled undergrowth, so we almost missed them. I was delighted to have discovered a new site with orchids growing undisturbed.

Some toads sat between the plants - beauty and the beasts. A group of bulbuls twittered overhead in the palms that swayed in the wind. A fort stood guard over the oasis, square against the sunny sky.

A small terraced field was planted with garlic and the large, spherical flower heads gleamed white in the gathering dusk. At the edge of the field was a vine with attractive, heart-shaped leaves, which I had only seen in pictures before. It is called *Pergularia tomentosa.* It was full of buds, some of which had unfolded to show a graceful, bell-shaped flower with dark green and brownish petals.

In the failing light we reached the orchid pond, where row upon row of beautiful fronds reflected in the dark still water. With the dusk, the bird-song had died down and the immense silence of the valley was broken only by the gentle rush of water running across the pebbles in the nearby wadi.

Musandam

Twice we had postponed a trip to the Musandam, waiting for the flowering season. As it turned out, we were lucky, for by postponing we had avoided rain, extreme cold, and thick fog. Now we started out on a clear, calm day.

We drove in easy stages, stopping frequently to investigate a plant, to have tea, or to admire a view. On the high plain near Masafi, we took a break to take a look at the annuals that covered the rocky ground. The small white lilies, *Asphodelus fistulosus,* grew in great numbers. *Tephrosia apollinea* bushes

Many different species of Praying mantis can be found in this area.

sported lush sprays of dark red pea blossoms. The yellow spikes of *Ochradenus aucheri* attracted dozens of brilliantly coloured butterflies and wasps.

Brilliantly coloured also was a small beetle that scurried among the seedlings at my feet. It had a bright red carapace with a black and white design on it that could have been American Indian art! It was a very active creature and would not stay still to be photographed.

When we found a second one, CC put them in the cool-box for a few minutes and then set them out on a tiny prostrate plant. The trifoliate leaves contrasted nicely with the gravel around it, while the minute yellow flowers at the center of the plant formed a colourful counterpoint for the two red bugs. The sun warmed them very quickly and soon they were on their way again.

The wind swayed the countless lilies and the sun lit up their fragile petals - a wonderful sight. But from the road you would hardly notice them at all. You had to be close, and at ground level, to enjoy the delicate beauty of this spring meadow in the desert.

We took the rough track through the wadi beyond Tabiyyah. This wadi is usually completely dry, but at one time huge amounts of water must have cascaded down, in order to create this magnificent gorge. On both sides the cliffs rose so steeply that the sunlight could not reach the bottom of the valley. We were kept busy pointing out to each other bizarre rock configurations in various browns, ochres and even reds. Where the wadi widened a small attempt at farming had created a few flat fields, which were now covered with weeds. While I admired the large blue flowers and yellow "apples" of a large *Solanum incanum* bush of the Nightshade family, CC discovered the deserted nest of a praying mantis. It looked a bit like a "gall" on a twig, but one made of styrofoam. Baby mantises, I was told, look very much like ants. CC had discovered that when he took a fresh "stryofoam" nest home one day, not knowing what it was, and left it in a drawer. Soon the drawer was swarming with ants, which on closer investigation turned out to be miniature mantises!

Beyond Dibba the road led through another gorge with steep sides. I was searching the higher regions of the rock face, for I had heard that the "stinking caralluma" occurs here. This is not an unwashed hermit, but a cactus-like milkweed with purplish-brown, bizarre flowers that smell like carrion. I did not find one, but a much more beautiful flower: a specimen of *Lavandula citriodora,* the lavender labiate flowers grouped together at the tip of a long slender stem.

We passed through the canyon. The road started to climb steeply through a series of hairpin curves. The mountain tops were veiled in white clouds. Here and there a settlement was just visible on the hillsides: very low structures built of the same rocks that surrounded them, which blended perfectly with their environment. A villager jumped from rock to rock along a track towards his farm, where several women and children closely followed our progress into their domain. When we stopped to look at a shrub, they called to us and waved.

The shrub that had caught our attention was spectacular: a large, very spiny bush with purplish-blue pea-flowers emerging from a bright red calyx. Lower down on the stems, the flowers had dropped off and the seeds were hidden inside the calices, which had become very large and balloon-like, varying in colour from red to pink to almost white. The microclimate inside these calices protects the seeds from extreme temperature fluctuations, and dissemination by wind is facilitated by their light weight. I identified the plant from pictures I had seen as *Astragalus fasciculifolius.*

There were a lot of little annuals hidden among the rocks: legumes with pink, mauve and bright yellow flowers appeared on plants with leaves of all shapes: trifoliate, serrated or feathered. The prettiest leaf by far was that of a little fern, which needed no flower to distinguish itself. I had read about this *Onychium divaricatum* and was delighted to find it. An even finer, almost hairy fern I could not immediately identify. A specimen that I picked was later discovered to be *Onychium melanolepis,* and this was the first time the plant was recorded in this region.

The view across the deep valleys to the other mountaintops was impressive. The barrenness of the mountains showed up the geological formations clearly. Sweeping curves, where layered sediments had been eroded away, led down to chasms so deep that the floors were lost in darkness.

Darkness was descending upon us quickly and we had to find a place to camp. Fearing that a mountaintop campsite might be too chilly, we descended into Wadi Bih and pitched camp there. The setting sun illuminated the mountain across the valley with a golden glow. A moringa tree spread its branches

In the wet mountains one can find mosses and lichens.

Astragalus fasciculifolius.

A *Moringa peregrina* tree spreads its flowering branches.

Dandelion and Stork's bill: *Reichardia tingitana* and *Monsonia nivea*.

Purple Sunbird in full plumage.

over our camp-fire, and its sweet-smelling blossoms were lit up by the dancing flames. A small hawk-moth started its evening rounds of the tephrosia bushes. Birds called in the hills around us for a while and then the quiet descended on the valley, while the night sky started to glitter with myriads of stars...

In the early morning a strange sound woke me up. A goat was observing me curiously from a rock high overhead, and appeared to be reporting his findings to his mate by muttering over his shoulder. In the early sunlight the rocks around me were not barren at all. Big boulders were festooned with garlands of greenery around their base and I was immediately intrigued by the unfamiliar shapes of the plants I saw. Everywhere dandelions were unfolding. These were of a species that grew very close to the ground. A rosette of prostrate leaves with a stemless flower of yellow with a dark red heart, rested directly on it. There were several annuals of about 15 cms in height; one had tiny red and yellow snapdragon flowers, another sported pale lavender ones and yet another had clusters of tiny white flowers grouped around the stems. Small Stork's bills were abundant with delicate pink flowers.

Some plants were overgrown with what looked like pieces of cotton wool. When I looked closely I saw that these little white globes were made up of tiny white and yellow flowers, belonging to a parasitic vine. They had various hosts, and I picked a branch of a tephrosia bush on which quite a few white dots were apparent. These were flower-heads and were attached directly to a leaf, with two air roots, one small and one longer, but without connections to other flower-heads of the same type. What a curious plant! Did the seeds germinate on the leaves of a host plant? Then why should one host plant be covered with the parasite and others be completely free? Later I asked an expert about it. He guessed from my description that it was a member of the Cuscuta family (*Cuscuta planiflora*) and told me that it actually starts life as a proper plant with roots and leaves. As soon as the tendrils, searching for a host plant, have latched on to one, its roots die down and it takes up a purely parasitic existence.

A couple of Purple Sunbirds flew busily to and fro between the trees, while a larger bird settled on a post only a few yards away. Its beautiful green feathers shimmered in the sunlight. It was my first really good view of the Little Green Bee-eater and I watched it for a long moment, before it flew off.

Heading home we drove through the mesquite forests near Digdaga. The mesquite tree (*Prosopis juliflora*) is not an indigenous tree, though I am not sure when and from where it was introduced. Certainly it is one of the most successful trees for the climate and conditions of this area. It can, for instance, tolerate the salinity of the soil far better than the (also imported) eucalyptus trees, which are dying everywhere due to the increased salt content of the soil after so many dry years. The mesquite can survive on dew alone for long stretches of time. If the air is dry, the leaves close tightly to conserve moisture. It is obviously not as popular with the camels as its relative, the ghaf (*Prosopis cineraria*) for one does not ever see a grazed mesquite.

On a sandy plain near Manama several arta bushes were showing off their delicate white blossoms with their flamboyant seed pods. One bush had both red, pink and whitish lampions, while another was adorned with very dark red ones, a colour that was almost black.

In a large grazed clump of *Rhanterium epapposum* a lizard sat sunning its long tailed body. It was dark brown, with a delicate speckled pattern along its back. It sat motionless throughout an extensive photo-session, moving only when I moved in to photograph it too closely.

Zoo walk

In a part of the Al Ain Zoo, nature has been given a chance to develop freely. A surrounding fence protects the area from being grazed by camels and goats, and its distance from the main zoo area prevents disturbance by people. It always amazes me that some people think desert hyacinths have been created only to be kicked over, but the large number of destroyed plants along the zoo paths bears witness to the fact!

One afternoon we made our way past the lion enclosure and spotted a few well-known weeds along the way: the yellow four-petalled flowers of *Dypterigium glaucum,* some heliotropes, and the white *Malva aegyptia* locally known as khubbayz (which means little loaf of bread) because of the shape of its seed pod.

A few new finds were recorded and collected. There was a yellow thistle, a flowering atriplex, and some species of launaea of the Daisy family. But the

The red lampions of arta.

A lizard sunning.

A species of Launaea.

Eremobium aegyptiacum - a spring ephemeral.

special find was a small crucifer, which only occurs after rain, when it erupts in great numbers, the fragile plants emerging straight from the sand. It flowers when it is only a few centimetres high, and bears fruit within a couple of weeks, so that its continued existence is ensured, even if the rest of the winter stays dry. If more rain falls, the plants develop further, even branching out and reaching a height of over 20 cms. It is called *Eremobium aegyptiacum*. The classicist among us translated the name: *eremos* means desert and *bium* is derived from *bios* which means life. 'Desert life' seems an apt name for this simple little plant with its quick life-cycle.

In a patch of *Tribulus terrestris* a large hole was visible among the roots. I took it to be a gerbil burrow, but then a sudden movement at the entrance caught my eye.

It turned out to be an elegant Domino beetle that lived there. Its Arabic name is umm-al' roob (which means mother-of-yoghurt), presumably referring to the white spots on its black back. It is a predator beetle, that hunts other insects for food. Even though it is quite common, I always enjoy seeing it, because of its nice markings.

The predator Domino beetle is locally called "umm-al-roob".

Mazyad

In December I had found a plant in the Mazyad oasis which was not flowering at the time. Since it was now spring and everything was in blossom, I wanted to go back to the site and find out what the flowers looked like. When I first saw this plant with its ferocious long spines and tiny leaves, it reminded me of an oversized fagonia species. But the black twisted seed pods guided me to a description in Loutfy Boulos' book *Weeds of Egypt*, and I decided it was *Alhagi maurorum*, "a common weed of irrigated areas and roadsides".

When I arrived at the site, however, the plants were not flowering. Instead they were all shrivelled up and dead-looking, not a green leaf or even a seed pod in sight. So this must be one of those rare plants that blossom during the hot months, and the seed pods, which I had found earlier, were not last year's but recent ones. Never mind, any excuse to come back to Mazyad from time to time is welcome!

In the back section of the oasis there were fallow fields on which a variety of wild flowers had sprung up. *Crotalaria aegyptiaca* and calotropis bushes were enormous here. On one crotalaria bush a great number of stunningly beautiful caterpillars were feeding. They were silvery grey marked with orange and black bands. A few weeks later, small polka-dotted day moths were laying eggs on the same bush, so we deduced that caterpillar and moth were of the same species, *Utetheisa pulchella*.

I was disappointed that there were so few of the ephemerals, the spring flowers, visible. But then, ephemeral is what they are: here today, gone tomorrow. They had already lived their short life, sprouted, flowered, seeded and died in a matter of weeks.

One small plant was unknown to me, and still quite green. It consisted of a rosette of oval leaves with wavy edges, and a number of inflorescences in between that looked like dandelions past their prime. But these flowers were all in the same stage of development - none "younger" or "older", no buds and no seeds. I dug one seedling out to put in the press and then discovered a strange feature. At the place where the tap-root of the plant dug into the sand, a sturdy wooden disc encircled the root. In fact, there were two long roots and they were threaded through a tiny hole in the centre of the disc

Utetheisa pulchella, a day-flying moth, has silvery caterpillars.

while the leaves of the plant rested on top. When I examined the disc closely, I realised it was one of the "flowers" that I had noticed between the leaves. Was it a seed pod rather than a flower? And what an extraordinary way for a plant to grow! What could be the purpose of the disc? Could it give the plant more stability in the loose sand in which it was growing?

Even though I found out the name of the plant - *Neurada procumbens* - I never discovered why the flower/seed-head, that acts as a base for the seedling, does not die off, after the plant has sprouted. Even much larger, older plants still have them.

Liwa

The high dunes at Liwa are most beautiful when seen from the south side with the late afternoon sun bringing out all the colours and contours. Because the prevailing wind is from the north, the concave, steep side of the sickle-shaped barchans is turned towards the south.

On both sides of the road were fenced areas with planted trees, and in between these grew an abundance of local wild plants and trees. We stopped when I spotted a particularly lush growth of *Tribulus deserti.* This zahra shrub, a favourite fodder of the oryx that once upon a time roamed these deserts, grows to a height of three feet, and has branches with feathered leaves speckled with yellow flowers shaped like single wild roses. The seeds are prickly globes, a bit like a small chestnut, but compartmented. Next to the tribulus bush, a nice stand of sedge waved in the breeze, and, a bit further on, I saw a huge bush which looked like the European broom. It had yellow flowers, like a broom-bush - but unlike it, in that they were tiny: three to four mm in diameter and star-shaped, clinging close to the branches. I had seen it in pictures, but never yet in reality: *Leptodenia pyrotechnica* (which sounds to me like Fireworks bush). The seed pods were long, especially taking into account the minute size of the flowers. They reached a length of 15 cms and were about the thickness of a finger.

Sharp ridges separate the convexities of a barchan dune from the sheer drops.

It took me a minute to recognise the next plant: an arta bush. The only arta that I had seen previously had been a bundle of dry sticks, decorated with the typical red-lampion seed pods and tiny white flowers. This one was a healthy looking dark green, with a few green-white lampions and no flowers. A nice steady drip of water makes all the difference.

This bush, *Calligonum comosum,* is an important plant of the desert. It has extremely long tap-roots and grows in dry places, where it acts as a sand-stabilizer. The thick woody branches serve as firewood and as such I had used it for camp-fires long before I knew what it was. I have been told that some part of the plant is used by the bedu as a spice for rice-dishes, but I still have to find out what part.

Kitnah

There are many tracks off the road from Al Ain to Sohar, which are worth exploring. On a cool Friday we had decided to look for the "stinking caralluma." This is a very odd and rather rare member of the Milkweed family. At first sight it resembles a cactus, but this it cannot be, since cacti are indigenous only to the Americas. Since it prefers rocky mountains as its habitat, I was interested when my friend R told me she had seen one near a wadi. So we had planned this trip at a time when the plant was supposed to be in full flower.

The road to the wadi wound through low hills with sparse vegetation and impressive rock formations. Every now and then the higher mountains of the Hajar range could be seen in the distance. Just before we reached a settlement, the track curved to the right and ended at the wadi's edge. We descended the steep bank to the water level and started walking upstream. The village on the left was dominated by the ruins of an old fort. The palm groves on the right were obviously of great age. The wadi was wide at this point, with several pools and water courses, some of which had been dammed and diverted.

A little further on, it narrowed to pass through a rocky gorge, where the water came down with force causing a spray of droplets to rain on the maidenhair ferns that quivered just above the water. Upstream from this gorge a large dam had been built of mud, and, behind it, quite a sizable lake had formed. The dam was covered with small weeds, which were taking advantage of the favourable combination of plentiful water and sunshine.

I recognised *Trigonella hamosa* with its clusters of tiny yellow flowers. Some stands of rushes were in flower, as were the many clumps of incense grass *(Cymbopogon parkeri)* and *Chloris virgata*. To enjoy the beauty of flowering grasses you really need a macrolens or magnifying glass.

One fragile-looking plant was new to me: it had shocking pink flowers, with pointed petals that curled into each other when the flower closed later in the day. The plant was barely 10 cms in height, and the flower was less than one cm in diameter, but there were so many flowers on each plant and the colour was so bright, that it was one of the more conspicuous flowers that I had seen in this area so far. (See P 27).

We came upon a stretch where a number of pools with different colours were strung like beads - turquoise, green, yellow, pure white, pink - depending on their depth and the algae or deposits they contained. A thick grove of palms and reed offered cool shade in which to enjoy this view. It was a perfect place to rest before we tackled the last part of our quest for the caralluma.

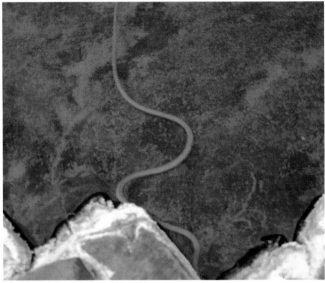
Wadi-racers are harmless water snakes.

When we continued our walk, we had to negotiate water-filled canyons. The scenery was spectacular: clear green pools between steep smooth rocks which continued up and up to great heights to meet the infinity of the cloudless sky.

We rounded a bend in the wadi and I jumped over to a rock in mid-stream. My movement disturbed a Wadi-racer, which lay snoozing peacefully in the sun. It zigzagged into the water, but since the pool was small, it had nowhere to hide. This gave us a good opportunity to have a close look at it. It is a sand-coloured snake with a small, streamlined head and (in this case) a three foot long unmarked body about as thick as a man's thumb. It is not harmful. Once, in another wadi, one was disturbed from its rock and slid into the water just as I swam past. It landed practically on top of me, but, even then, it did not bite but fled as fast as it could. So did I!

We had reached our destination, but to my dismay the exact location of the caralluma plant was on top of a 30-foot hill — and the first half was vertical rock.

"It's easy", said my friend - who climbs rocks like a mountain goat. In fact, she was already halfway up before she realised that I had a problem. "You can do it!"

Even if the first statement was not true, the second turned out to be - and finally, there was the caralluma. And not just one, but half a dozen plants. Thick grey stems with scalloped edges grew straight out of the rock and were crowned with either buds or flowers past their prime. Not one plant showed a flower in full bloom and the carrion-like smell, which is described in the books, was not in evidence. The plant was a lot smaller than I had imagined it to be from the pictures I had seen. This is often the case with the inconspicuous desert plants, since close-up photography shows up details which can hardly be seen with the naked eye.

We took pictures and a cutting which caused the white latex to well up from the plant. The wind whistled through the gorge and threatened to blow us off the hill. Climbing down is harder than up, at least if you want to arrive in one piece, but with careful coaching I made it to the Wadi-racer's level again. The snake had found a safer hide-out and we went to look for a deeper pool for a swim and a picnic.

Bahrain

At last I have seen a gazelle in the wild! Unfortunately is was not in the UAE, though there are occasional sightings of wild Arabian gazelles in the hills around Al Ain and in Jebel Ali. The gazelle we saw - from our car during a trip around Bahrain - was a lone male Sand gazelle, larger and lighter-coloured than the Arabian gazelle. He had crossed the road a few hundred yards ahead of us and was walking calmly along the path at the foot of some hills, even standing still for minutes on end to watch us as intently as we watched him.

Bahrain, which at first sight seems so flat, so cultivated and unpromising for nature-lovers, provided us with a number of rare treats. Its lush green belt at the northern end of the island is a haven for birds, both resident and migratory. Here I got my first view of the beautiful Blue-cheeked Bee-eater, a medium-sized bird with a narrow head and a longish tail. Quite a few were sitting on electricity lines, looking for prey. Taking wing, they would flutter frantically at first and then swoop down towards insects they had spotted, their brilliant green and brown plumage glinting in the sun.

Near a broombush *(Leptodenia pyrotechnica)* we saw a flock of Collared Doves, larger and paler than the more ubiquitous Palm Doves.

A rocky outcrop was investigated in the course of our search for reptiles. One rock hid a large predator beetle, the Domino beetle, one of the more spectacular bugs that I had seen so far. It has an ant-shaped black body, with the surface of its back ribbed in black and spotted with white.

Another group of rocks lay tumbled together to form a shady cave, which was inhabited by a young Desert or Cape hare. It crouched, frozen with fear, for a long moment, before it regained the use of its limbs to dart off in zigzags across the plain. Later in the day we saw some adult hares, that were less shy - we could approach one quite closely to take pictures.

The next day, we set out after a leisurely breakfast to look for Spiny-tailed lizards, or 'dthub'.

In the area, which was known to be their habitat, we saw them almost immediately. They were sitting near the entrance to their holes, not daring to venture out yet, since they were still cold and therefore slow. When we approached them they retreated immediately into their burrows. There were many of them in different sizes up to over two feet in length.

The area resembled the gopher towns I had seen in the prairies of North America: small brown heads sticking up between low bushes and scattered rocks.

As the sun rose higher their colour changed from brown-grey to light sulphury yellow, and, when they were warmed, they ventured from their burrows to forage. We saw one nibbling a fagonia species. Many of the turnsole bushes also had lizard tracks around them, and my friends said they had once seen one with zygophyllum leaves dangling from its mouth.

Now that the 'spinies' (as they were affectionately called) were out in the open, we managed to catch first one, then another. It was my first time ever to handle a reptile and I was surprised at how warm and pleasant it felt. We put one down near a bush to photograph, and it stayed put, hissing at us and inflating its belly to intimidate us. Then we placed the two we had caught close together - but that galvanised both of them into action. They ran off in opposite directions as fast as their feet could carry them! Clearly they are not gregarious animals!

A little further on we saw another one and CC gave chase. Just as he overtook it, the lizard jumped sideways into a pipe-coupling that lay rusting among the rocks. No matter how hard we shook it, it would not budge - it knew it had a good hiding place!

Another young specimen ambled slowly across the road. We stopped the car to watch it. When it reached the other side, it stopped and turned around to take a good look at us from a distance of a yard or so. Then, as if it suddenly realised that it did not like the looks of us at all, it whirled around and took off at such speed that its legs looked like blurs on either side of its body. Its sudden panic was comical indeed!

We had seen one small Snub-nosed lizard which was much too fast to be caught, but there were other kinds that could be approached by stealth: agamas were sunning themselves in zygophyllum bushes and were caught quite easily. As we had been told that they turn their scales into brilliant colours when they are angry or "in heat", we teased our captive gently by blowing on its head until it responded. The head turned turquoise blue, while the pouch at its throat became a dark violet. The inside of the mouth and the tail turned orange.

Uromastix microlepis - the gentle dragon of the desert.

A while later we saw one which had turned its colours on full blast on behalf of the opposite sex. CC approached it carefully and skilfully, and we watched in fascination as the reptile faded its colours gradually, trying to merge into the background to become invisible to the approaching predator. To no avail, for CC caught him with ease. After we had taken our pictures and were about to let the agama go, it got its own back on its captor and bit him hard, several times, before zipping off across the plain, faster than the speed of light (or so it seemed!).

The pleasure of this morning was spoiled by the realization that these fascinating creatures may not be around much longer to be enjoyed by others after us. Industry and housing are encroaching upon their habitat and they are being hunted for gourmet food - and for kicks. On one stretch of road, a kilometre or so in length, we counted nine dead lizards, all killed by cars. Since these animals were mainly light yellow, it meant that they were killed as they lay sunning themselves on the warm asphalt at midday, when they could easily have been seen and spared. But people in fast cars do not always care enough, it seems, and so these creatures which have lived on the island for many millions of years, may not see the end of this century unless something is done to save them.

Blue-headed agama.

Chapter 3

MAY
JUNE

The hot months have arrived. Although trips into the desert are still feasible, it is important to take plenty of drinking water, headgear and sun-tan lotion as temperatures can reach 40°C at midday. The evenings are the best times now. It is light till 7.30 pm and the temperatures at night are wonderful, a perfect time for outdoor camping. It is great to sleep on the soft sand of the dunes, to watch the brilliant stars rotate over your head, and to wake up in the morning with the tracks of dozens of little (and large!) desert animals around you.

This is also the time when visits to the East and West coast beaches are fun. One can go there all year round, but at the change of the seasons one can have undesirable encounters with stingrays, while in the winter the water can be quite chilly, and poisonous sea snakes tend to come closer inshore.

Dibba

I still remember my delight at seeing the mountains of the Musandam rising steeply from the plain of the Dibba fault and I was looking forward to showing this magnificent view to my friend. It was a hazy day however, and we could barely make out the peaks or Jebel Qahwah as they merged with the pale blue sky.

The road plunged down to sea level, and soon we reached the outskirts of Dibba. An Indian Roller was perched on an electricity wire along the roadside. We stopped the car just underneath it.

A car is a great hide from which to observe birds. They will often pay no attention to vehicles but would fly away immediately if approached on foot. This bird was unconcernedly staring across the gravel plain, now preening his blue-and-russet plumage, then cocking his head to observe an interesting detail on the ground.

We reached the coast and turned left to have a look at Dibba town, which has the distinction of being divided into three municipalities: one part belongs to the Emirate of Sharjah, one to that of Fujairah, and the northern part lies in Oman.

As we skirted the oasis a large bird wheeled in the sky and soon we saw more. They were House Crows and we had not seen them anywhere else in the Emirates before.

In the main street a dozen of them had collected around a garbage container, where some donkeys

The feathers of the Indian Roller are brilliantly coloured.

The wadis have a lot of greenery.

House crows are gradually enlarging their habitat and have already reached Dubai from the East coast.

Socotra Cormorant drying its wings (Photo: M West).

were foraging too. Every now and then a bird would hop on to a donkey's back for a ride. Some crows were sitting in a row on the edge of the container. They hopped sideways until they reached the slanted edge and then they slid down, till they dropped off, seemingly just for fun. We watched their antics for a while before continuing on to the Corniche.

The blue sea looked invitingly cool and I was impatient to go for a swim. But we were stopped by an exciting sight, a swarm of hundreds of cormorants dipping in and out of the water, obviously attracted by schools of fish. With the binoculars we could make out that they were all black: Socotra Cormorants, which have breeding colonies on the islands in the Straits of Hormuz. It was fantastic to see this great flock flying back and forth in a seemingly endless stream. Whenever they landed on the water, they were temporarily invisible, but soon they would be up in the air again - a black smudge against the blue of sea and sky.

Dhow trip

At Dibba harbour we met a group of friends who had camped on the beach. We had rented a couple of dhows for a boating trip along the Musandam coast. As we waited for the stragglers to arrive, we were entertained by the activities of the local people, who were selling fish, fruit and vegetables. At the same time we were providing them with entertainment as they regarded our picnic boxes, sun-hats and tele-lenses.

As soon as we had settled on the decks of the dhows, we departed, heading north. It was an overcast day and the tops of the mountains were hidden in haze. There was a moderate swell and it was pleasant to rock back and forth with the movement of the ship. Suddenly there was a splash to starboard... and another .... and another! Dolphins! What a wonderful sight to see them frolicking in the waves. Then, to our delight, a cloud of silver emerged from the sea, glittering in the sunshine before splashing back into the water. Flying fish were being chased out of their element by predators down below.

The coast on our left looked impressive but inhospitable. From the map we knew that there were many inlets and even some villages, but from here it was impossible to see them. When we sailed closer to the shore, we came upon one such inlet. Beautiful rock formations rose steeply from the sea, with sparse vegetation clinging to ledges and in crevices. As we sailed into the hidden bay, I could understand why this coast was called the Pirate Coast. This was a perfect place to hide from pursuit or to lie in ambush!

A few hundred yards along was a rocky beach with a small settlement, dominated by a huge water tank. The dhows anchored and most of us jumped overboard without checking about how to get back. As the ships turned out to have no ladders we were to regret that impulsive action! The water was pleasantly cool, but not very clear, due to surface pollution-so the pleasure of swimming was spoilt by being covered with an oily film of dirt. Fortunately nature provided some entertainment in the form of two large turtles, which swam fearlessly among us. One had a flipper missing and had some difficulty swimming properly. Their shields were encrusted with barnacles, which had had plenty of time to grow, since these animals must have been a hundred years old or more, judging by their size.

After spending considerable effort in getting everybody back on board, we steamed south again. The sky had darkened into what looked like rain clouds and the sunlight drew a ribbon of light on the slate-grey waves. The high-pooped dhow was dwarfed by the immense cliffs that rose from the sea. How I would have loved to see that ship with sails.

On our left the great flock of cormorants flew by in an endless formation. The water foamed when they splashed down - then they rose again, back and forth over their fishing ground. In spite of the oily detritus that we had encountered, bird and marine life in the Strait of Hormuz still seemed all right - but would they last?

Khor Fakkan

The mountains that guard the Batinah coast rose in rows of ever darkening shades of grey behind the palm groves near Khor Fakkan. This same view must have warmed the hearts of the 17th century sailors as they made their way along this coast to the Far East. Ruins of an old fort were silhouetted against the sky just above the picturesque small mosque that is reported to be the oldest in the Emirates.

We reached the beach in time for a walk in the last light of the day. The tide was going out and had left the rocks dry, so that we could explore them at leisure.

They were literally crawling with snails. At first we thought there were many different kinds, but closer examination revealed only two species: a slate-grey truncated snail, and a rounder type, which occurred with many different patterns and colours: bold stripes, dots, or zigzags. There were other creatures clinging to the rocks: sharp-edged barnacles, purple-and-white oyster shells, limpets and chitons. With some effort, CC dislodged one of this latter species to have a closer look at it. The chiton is a very primitive mollusc, with a jointed oval shell, edged with a dark, brush-like fringe. They scrape the rocks with a file-like tongue, rasping off vegetation. When we put it in a Masafi bottle with seawater, it curled up slowly, looking a bit like an underwater armadillo.

Some snail shells moved a bit faster and more jerkily than others, and these turned out to be inhabited by hermit crabs. These little creatures use empty shells as homes. When shells are not available, they find substitutes. We once found one which had taken up its abode in a Johnny Walker bottle top!

The next morning the beach was littered with dozens of large starfish. They were some 35 cms in diameter with seven tentacles, striped in beige and dark brown. I did not realize it at the time, but the seven arms made these starfish something special. Apparently most starfish have either five or a multiple of five.

Sand dollars abounded also. When we examined one closely we decided that we did not really know anything about them, and this led to a perusal of available books during the following days. We discovered that sand dollars are a type of sea-urchin, flat as a pancake, and covered with minute spines, which are soft like felt. With the sharp edge of the hard skeleton, they can burrow in the sand either obliquely, to bury themselves underneath the surface in order to hide; or vertically, with their bodies perpendicular to the movement of the waves, so that the food-laden water can pass through the holes that perforate the top of the shell in the shape of a five-petalled flower.

The underside of the sand dollar is patterned in a lacework of branching canals, presumably to guide the waterflow through the entire organism. Unfortunately the skeleton is quite brittle and I did not find one that was completely intact.

Now that the tide was coming in and the waves were washing over the night's deposits, I turned my attention to the area more inland, which I had not yet

Boerhavia diffusa: a 3mm flower head.

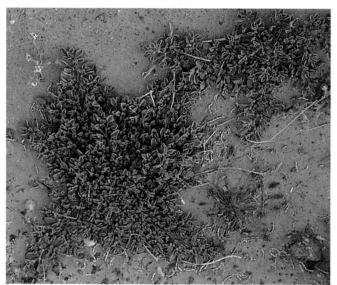

A perfect specimen of Aizoon canariense.

Starfish sometimes litter the coast.

explored. The most conspicuous example of plant life was the goat creeper or *Ipomoea biloba*. This plant, a member of the Bindweed family, has been imported from Pakistan and is so hardy that it will grow almost anywhere. Its vines, with purple-blue flowers, cover large areas of beach and garden. Another plant had pale-blue flowers with calices covered with fine white hairs. This turned out to be *Salvia macilanta*, which is often found on the slopes of the inland mountains. This one, with the blue sea for background, provided excellent photographic material. The small flowers of the arid areas are so difficult to photograph that one is always trying to get a better picture, always hoping for the perfect shot.

If I thought the salvia flower was small, the next plant proved even tinier! A dark-leaved ground-covering plant carried minute crimson flower heads and dark red berry-like seeds; *Boerhavia diffusa* it is called. One flower head that consisted of half a dozen separate flowers was no larger than three mm across!

Now that I had my nose really close to the ground I saw another plant that might have escaped my notice otherwise. I recognised it immediately by its growth pattern: a five-pointed star! Between the succulent leaves dozens of five-petalled white flowers and pinkish fruits were hidden. A perfect specimen of *Aizoon canariense.*

Sharm

Where the falaj curves around the bottom of the hill, the shade is cool and dark. Dozens of toads jumped away at our approach. Of course I used to call them frogs, like everyone else, until it was pointed out to me that there are no frogs in the UAE. The difference between toads and frogs lies mainly in the skin on their back, which in the case of the former is tough and lumpy. The small streams were lined with maiden hair fern *(Adiantum capillus-veneris)* and at one point, where a trickle of water gurgled down a pile of rocks, the ferns grew so abundantly that a natural rock garden had been formed. Small flowers grew everywhere. The yellow cups of the *Sida urens* peeped from between their floor-covering leaves. Near the water's edge small groups of *Lippia nodiflora* raised their proud lavender heads. There was a small, blue-white cup-shape flower that looked a bit like an anemone, which is called *Bacopa monnieri.* Tephrosia bushes grew to a respectable height and many species of grass gave shelter to crickets and grasshoppers. A wild fig tree spread stunted leaves towards the light at the edge of the oasis, and higher up on the hill a dense grove of lime trees mingled its scent with that of the sidr tree flowers that were blooming abundantly. A large yellow and black butterfly danced in and out of the bushes - a Lime Swallow-tail.

Ochre wasps were busy foraging among the moist pebbles in the stream. A small, almost black, butterfly made a graphic contrast with the unsullied white of a jasmine flower.

The village behind the oasis had been deserted quite a while before. Some of the houses and courtyards had carved doors that were still intact. Bits and pieces of household goods were strewn all around. I picked up a child's tiny leather sandal, and a small bracelet woven out of palm tree fibres. Several loosely constructed barasti huts dotted the area and behind them the brown hills lay hot and silent in the midday sun. A strong breeze whistled through some ropes which were strung across a courtyard. The atmosphere was eerie, like the set of a western movie just before the enemy's attack.

I tried to imagine living here, wedged between the hot rocks and the swaying green palms, in this silence and solitude. But of course, there would have been the shouts of children, the noise of cattle, and the hum of daily life in the houses and huts. But no

A Hume's Wheatear visiting its water place.

clamour of air-conditioners, radios, cars and machinery disturbed this day—only the buzz of a million flies.

Dragonflies can reach speeds of 50 kms/hour.

Assubaithi Revisited

At 6.30 in the morning it was still wonderfully cool. The air was clear and the mountains were bright on the horizon. The dirt track towards the mountains led me through the dry wadi bed to the edge of the oasis. There were a number of plants here that I wanted to see again. A *Boerhavia elegans*, which I had noticed before when it was a seedling, had now grown into a good-sized plant. It had a rosette of dark green leaves close to the ground, from which delicate red stems rose up, ending in panicles of tiny pink flowers. It is an impossible plant to photograph, because the hairlike stems tremble continuously. The Arab name is hadimdam which is supposed to mean "red smoke" or "pink cloud" and refers to the impression one gets when one sees this plant from a distance; a pink haze blurring the rocky background.

Close by grew a ground-covering plant which I had taken for a desert squash when I had seen it before. Now it had fruits and I realised that I had been wrong. The fruits were quite a bit smaller than the yellow tennis balls of the desert squash. They were plum-sized and had soft spines. This was *Cucumis prophetarum*.

The thistles I had noticed here before had grown to a man-sized height, and most of the flower heads had already gone to seed. I was surprised to see that the *Cleome glaucescens* plants, which had been plentiful in February, where completely gone - only some straw-like matter indicated where they had been.

On the other hand, an eyelash plant (*Blepharis ciliaris)*, which I had not noticed there before, was now conspicuous with dozens of pale blue flowers peeking between the spiny upper leaves. The only plant unchanged was the senna plant *(Cassia italica)* with profuse yellow flowers, at the same time growing the first green curved seed pods that would later become black. This plant is a powerful cathartic and the seeds are used in many countries in the world as a laxative.

In the oasis the seasonal changes were also apparent; no more fragrant scent of lemon blossoms, but shrubs heavy with green fruits of lime, lemon and pomegranate. The camel's eyes were all gone and in their place now grew some everlasting composites: *Gnaphalium luteo-album*. The lush ground cover beneath the palms had disappeared and now the ground was littered with yellow and dark red dates, of which huge bunches were suspended in the trees above. Invisible birds chattered and chirped everywhere.

In the half-empty reservoir at the end of the falaj dozens of toads were loafing in the shallow water. As I sat down to watch a couple in close embrace, a huge blue dragonfly settled on the cemented edge of the pond. The sunlight bounced off its iridescent wings and put a sparkle in its huge pale eyes. My macrolens showed up every detail of his fragile body. Every now and then it would fly off, only to settle down again close by at a slightly different spot, so that I was able to take pictures in many different poses. I never met a more cooperative insect!

I walked on, following the falaj which curved along the side of the mountain. I rounded a corner and stopped in my tracks. A Hume's Wheatear was drinking at the falaj. This strikingly beautiful black and white bird had selected a spot next to an oleander bush, which carried a profusion of pink flowers. Behind the bird a large stand of maidenhair fern hung over the edge of the stream. The colours and the composition were wonderful. I stood and watched till the bird flew away. Then I chose a shady spot and sat down with the tele-lens focused on the watering place to wait to see if the bird would come back. He did, after a while, bringing a sand-coloured female. They sat on either side of the falaj and went into the water for a quick dip—but they were gone before I could focus properly. The water drops fell off their wings, sparkling like diamonds, as they dived side by side into the ravine.

Nothing happened for a long time, then a flock of small, beige birds tumbled through the palm leaves right in front of me. One sat so close that I could clearly see the pink inside of its mouth. I wondered if it was panting from the heat or with excitement.

When I looked back at the falaj, the wheatear was back and this time he stayed long enough for the shutter to click him into immortality!

Summer outings

We turned off the road into the bowl of Fossil Valley, heading towards an area where I wanted to hunt for a reported fossil of a fish's complete backbone.

Fossil Valley is not so much a valley as a ridge, curving around what must have been a bay some 60 million years ago. The mile-long ridge is made up of a solid sediment of marine deposits. Even though many visitors have searched its slope for the last few years, there are still many fossils to be found such as sea-urchins, pieces of corals and whelks, (some quite large in size), bi-valves and gastropods. At one time I found two structures that looked like canine teeth, which turned out to be a special kind of coral.

I pointed out some shell imprints to my companion and picked up one rock for a better look. A soft hiss alerted me - I had uncovered the hiding place of a baby Sawscale viper. The tiny creature was trying to intimidate me by rubbing its scales together to make the shhhh sound. When we started to take pictures, it repeatedly lunged with lightning speed at the camera, the small triangular head poised like an arrowhead on its beautifully marked body. We watched as it slithered away among the rocks to seek a new hiding place. The incident had once more

Baby Sawscale viper about to strike.

Ducrosia anethifolia is a strong-smelling herb.

The Monitor lizard is the largest reptile of the desert.

Just a few of the more than 300 species of bees and wasps of the UAE.

impressed upon me the need to be aware of the small dangers of the desert. If you do not watch where you put your hands and feet, you are liable to get bitten or stung with uncomfortable consequences!

The first person in our group to reach the row of cliffs overhanging the slope, started to explore the bizarre caves that occur there. Soon, an excited cry drew us towards one of these caves. It was not the fossilized fish skeleton that had been found, but a small bat which had found refuge there from the blistering sun. It was hanging upside down with its flying membranes spread out - a cooling mechanism? This species of bat, which we have also found in the Hajar mountains and in caves on the Musandam, has an unusual feature: the tail is not incorporated into the flying membrane between its hind legs, as is the case in most species of bat, but extends a good three inches outward.

As usual, my eye was more geared to plants than fossils. An unusual small plant, *Ducrosia anethifolia*, was flowering with tiny umbels - and when I picked a twig for the plant press, a pungent herbal smell became apparent.

We continued on our way to Sharm, turning back to the main unpaved road to Mahdah. Almost immediately I skidded the car to a halt again. On the road lay the largest lizard I had ever seen in the wild. Sadly, it was dead, run over by a car. The animal was over three feet from the tip of its nose to the end of its tail.

I recognised it right away as a Monitor lizard as there is no other lizard of this size in the Emirates. It was the first one I had ever seen.

It was hard to believe that this killing was unavoidable as the road was wide at this point.

The falaj at Sharm was flowing strongly - there was more water than I had ever seen before. There were also more wasps. I distinguished at least three different kinds: the common ochre yellow one, the brown and yellow *Vespa orientalis* and a black one with red wings and a thin elongated body. They were drinking in droves at the water's edge, sometimes landing on top of each other in their eagerness to get to the water. Dragonflies in brilliant colours sat on twigs overhanging the stream, and dozens of toads in all sizes jumped away at our approach.

There was an unusual fruit tree growing beside one of the houses. I had passed the tree before without noticing it, but now it was full of fruit that had a delicious sweet smell. Plum-sized, they were smooth and round like eggs and had a delicate peach colour. An unusual feature was the way the fruit was attached to the branches. The calyx enveloped the fruit like a dunce's cap and had the same smooth, leathery texture as the fruit itself. From a specimen I found later in another plantation, the tree was identified as *Cordia myxa* - but I have never seen the fruits in the suq yet!

Another bush was bearing fruit nearby: a large *Calotropis procera*, or Sodom's apple, had both flowers and seed pods. The flowers are miracles of geometry. When still in bud, they are pentagonal boxes of white velvet tinged with purple. Then, the petals fold out, their tips a dark purple, surrounding a pentagonal pistil, which is light green and glossy like porcelain. From the middle of each side of the pistil, dark purple stamens lie against the white bases of the flower's petals.

The flowers of Calotropis procera are miracles of geometry and the fruit is quite beautiful inside.

The fruit is even more intriguing, if you take the trouble to open one. Even though they are at least 10 cms long and three cms wide, they are surprisingly hard to find, if you only look at the shrub casually. Here in the UAE, they look like plump bananas, but from pictures and stories I gather that in North Africa they are more similar to apples, hence the common name Sodom's apple. Inside the soft green shell an intricate pattern is revealed. Each seed is shaped like a fish-scale and lies tightly against the next, attached by a silvery thread to the common core of the pod. When the pod bursts, the light seed will float away, carried by its parachute thread. It is a successful mechanism, judging by the fact that this is one of the most common bushes of all in North Africa and the Middle East.

Khutwa in summer

The day was hazy and the mountain range we were heading for was invisible until we were less than a few kilometres away. The alluvial plains, previously covered with the bobbing heads of the yellow spring crucifers, were now barren.

As usual, the first sight of Khutwa oasis, its verdant palm groves splashed between the rust brown mountains, drew a gasp of surprise from my companions. The groves were busy with local people tending the date palms, heavy with ripening fruit. We chatted a bit and some of the ladies were

Nerium oleander flowers the year round.

intrigued that we thought their nakheel worth taking pictures of; but they did not mind as long as they themselves did not figure in any photographs.

When we had passed through the groves, we descended to the gorge, where water was flowing noisily 20 metres or so below us. One little bridge, made of four, loose-lying palm trunks, was still the only way across the canyon to the island plateau between the two arms of the wadi. Having learned how to cross it without my knees turning to jelly, I now took great delight in daring the others to cross. Not many took up the challenge, and so we continued along the edge of the gorge, enjoying the spectacular view of the canyon.

Several shallow pools on top of the plateau were all that remained of the recent rains. Some oleander bushes were flowering copiously and in the barren surroundings, their green and pink colours stood out as on a surrealistic painting. A couple of Lime swallow-tails fluttered by and settled on a patch of mud nearby. They unrolled their long probosces and started drinking. We closed in slowly for some photographs, crawling on all fours on the hot rocks. As I focused the tele-lens on the insect, I noticed that large drops of clear liquid splashed down from the tip of its abdomen. Every three or four seconds a drop was secreted. Surely the butterfly could not drink that much liquid and turn it into urine in such a short time span? Then I remembered that I had just read something about this phenomenon in one of David Attenborough's books. He had observed it in Swallow-tails in Paraguay and surmised that they were filtering minerals, rather than just drinking. CC had also seen it in Africa, where butterflies congregate on river banks where cattle have been drinking and urinating, or where women have been washing clothes.

By now my eyes were filling up with salty sweat that caused me to wipe my face - and that distracted the butterflies sufficiently for them to disappear into the palm groves.

A sidr tree nearby reverberated with the strident song of a dozen cicadas. Summer was really here!

A natural botanical garden

I had noticed a narrow strip of desert along the road, where the greenery seemed to be more lush than usual. The area was located in a depression off a roundabout, and a broken water main explained the abundance of flowering plants. A fast little lizard flitted away before I could see what it was. It disappeared among the tangle of roots of a *Hammada elegans* bush. In this part of the area all the plants seemed to have yellow flowers. *Tribulus terrestris*, desert squash and *Portulaca oleracea*, which is locally sold as a salad green, all looked lush. Another lizard started from its resting place, but this one was much slower and I thought I recognised it by its smooth shiny skin as a sand skink. I followed it and when I came too close, it confirmed my identification by disappearing into the sand like a conjurer's trick.

I had now reached a different part of the "garden", where all the plants seemed to be purple-flowering. I saw numerous *Polygala erioptera*, with its tiny winged flowers. A nice specimen of the indigo plant was covered with its blood red pea flowers. The rather rare *Taverniera eagyptiaca* showed its veined fruit wings, that looked like insect wings.

Two different ground-covering euphorbias had flowers so small that they could only be distinguished with a magnifying glass. Some convolvulus and *Aerva javanica* gleamed white against the red soil. Two enormous senna plants, that had sprays of yellow flowers and curved black seed pods, were the largest plants around, while the lemon yellow flowers of the Arabian primrose were the brightest.

As I walked back I saw yet another lizard, and this one was at least a foot long. It ran away but stopped at the foot of an acacia tree and sat there as I approached, slowly. It was a Toadheaded agama, with beautiful markings on its back and tail. It was so handsome, that I wondered if it had just shed its skin. It posed willingly, keeping a wary eye on me.

Later, when I sat down to record what I had seen, it turned out that I had seen 53 species of plants and grasses on a strip of land, no larger than a city garden!

The butterfly bush

The roadsides of Al Ain are green and full of pleasant surprises for a naturalist on a hot afternoon, since one can explore from the cool confines of an air-conditioned car. I drove slowly, noticing as I went the different plants. *Salvadore persica* was ubiquitous. This is the shrub that provides the local "tooth-brushes" that one can buy in the suq. They produce sprays of berries that are decorative, since each berry is placed on a separate stalk and has a different size and colour, ranging from apple green through all shades of pink to dark blue and black. I have always noticed a peculiar smell, like that of a fox or a skunk, wherever these shrubs grow, but I have not been able to trace it to a specific part of the plant.

Between the toothbrush plants grew large tufts of sedge, with their decorative seeds already turning black. Saltbushes were well represented, and the spiky *Ochradenus baccatus* reached enormous sizes.

The only flowering plant at this time of the year was the fragile looking *Dipterygium glaucum*. This plant is almost like a grass, in that the long stems (up to one metre) have such small leaves that they are hardly noticeable. The flowers are pale yellow, clinging close to the stems, with the four petals curving slightly back from the long stamens. The seed pods, which often occur at the same time as the flowers, are crinkled oval boxes.

One bush was so large, that I stopped to have a closer look. As I approached it, it seemed to come alive. I watched in amazement as dozens of small butterflies detached themselves from the flowers,

The Sand fish's streamlined body enables it to swim underneath the surface of the sand like a fish in water.

only to settle again in a never ending dance among the sprays of flowers. There seemed to be two different kinds, but they could be males and females of the same species. Predominant were the larger orange-tipped ones, which had hind wings with black markings. The underside of the wings was lemon yellow with two black spots. The smaller type was a less pronounced yellow with no clear black markings. They fluttered restlessly in and out of the tangle of stems, groggy on nectar. The mercury must have been hitting the mid-40s then and it seemed almost impossible that fragile creatures like these could survive this heat, but maybe the high humidity helped. In any case, I was looking at something of rare beauty and I did not tire of watching the display.

The Butterfly bush.

Manna

The road from Al Ain to Abu Dhabi stretched interminably in front of me. To relieve the tedium I looked at the road's central reservation to see what grew there between the oleanders. The most obvious were the two foot long black stalks of dead desert hyacinths. They grow in circles around the oleanders, on which they live as parasites. Large zygophyllum bushes with their apple green succulent leaves contrasted nicely with the greygreen of *Pennisetum divisum*, a grass species that grows to an enormous size here. But the most attractive were the buttercup yellow flowers of the large tribulus. Each waving stem with pinnate leaves sported a rose-like flower at its very end, all turned towards the sun.

Suddenly a bush with large spots of orange colour caught my eye. I stopped at the side of the road and walked back to have a look. It was a low shrub with

A yellow beetle feeds on Tribulus flowers.

feathered leaves that resemble a ghaf or mesquite. The orange-pink seed pods were a bizarre bulbous shape like small potatoes, which did not resemble the seed pods of the mesquite or ghaf in the least. Still, it turned out to be related: *Prosopis farcta*.

Now that I was out of the car, I noticed another flash of colour, which I could not have seen while driving. This was a low bush with purple flowers, and I was delighted to find it. It was the *Alhagi maurorum* which I had visited many times in Mazyad, but had not seen in flower until now. Normally an unattractive plant, it was now really beautiful with masses of pink pea flowers between the spiky leaves.

An interesting fact is mentioned in one of my plant books: "The plant is renowned for its exudation - no doubt stimulated in hot dry weather by insect punctures - of a sugary sap, which dries into small brownish lumps of manna" (Townsend and Guest, 1974, quoted in *Weedflora of Egypt* by Loutfy Boulos).

Since I was not aware of this characteristic at the time, I did not look for the manna. I was attracting a lot of attention, there on the central reservation, so I decided to go back to Mazyad soon to spend more time with this interesting weed.

Cassia italica, the senna plant.

Chapter 4

JULY

AUGUST

The Cicada seems to have a seventh leg: its stylette drilled into the tree to sip the juices.

These months are the hottest with temperatures reaching 43°C, even at night there is little relief from the heat. Only "mad dogs and Englishmen" - and a few naturalists - still go on hikes and then only in the early morning.

Some plants are still flowering: *Tephrosia apollinea* and the eyelash plant, *Blepharis ciliaris,* can be found with flowers at any time of the year. The caper in the mountains flowers only now, but climbing up to see it is a bit of an effort. This is the time to carry out nature studies around the house!

Summer singer

I remember my first encounter with the cicada a few years ago. I walked past a small sidr tree, which seemed to reverberate with sound. I approached the tree and immediately all sound stopped. But I had seen no movement, so the creatures must still be there. I waited for a few minutes and, one after the other, they started up again. Guided by sound, my eyes searched the branches, but did not see anything except leaves and thorns. The noise was so loud, I had to be standing nose to nose with the producer of it, but there was still no sign of him. Then I came too close, for with a sudden whirring of wings, he flew off. When he settled on a more distant twig, I finally knew what to look for and immediately I could spot a dozen or so of the insects clinging to the branches. Their colouring blended so well with the bark that I had taken them for stubs and knots of the tree! I put the close-up lens on my camera and zeroed in on one that sat in an accessible place. Even when I approached quite closely, he did not move. His carapace was boldly marked in earth colours and veiled with gauze wings, which were outlined with distinct dark veins.

In profile, another striking feature appeared: he seemed to have an extra, seventh leg between his front legs. I looked closely and noticed that this was actually a mouth part, which was extending straight down into the branch he was sitting on. It was obviously used for drinking the tree's juices, and it looked for all the world as if he were sipping cola through a straw. That explained why he was so slow to fly away when I approached. It would take time to disengage this drilling instrument.

The ripe fruits of the desert squash look like yellow tennis balls.

I could not determine how the insects produced their loud song, but the encyclopaedia provided an answer. At the base of the abdomen, on the male cicada only, a special tough area is made to vibrate at about 4,500 cycles per second. The hearing organs of both males and females are also located near the base of the abdomen.

Eggs are laid on low branches or in the soil at the base of a food tree. When they hatch, the larvae dig in among the roots of the tree and live there throughout the various stages of their development - sometimes for many years. Eventually they emerge and sit on a twig to shed their last "nymphal" skin and the adult insect emerges.

Nocturnal animals

The low sand dunes below Jebel Hafeet are densely covered with shrubs and samr trees. This area, belonging to the Al Ain Zoo, is protected, and provides a wonderful habitat for the shy nocturnal animals of the desert.

As we strolled through the pulicaria and hammada bushes, a sudden movement at the foot of a large caligonum plant caught our eye.

"A gerbil", whispered CC, as we froze. I could barely see the outline of a small head and the gleam of a beady eye. We stayed motionless, trying to even breathe shallowly, waiting for the creature to regain confidence and emerge from its burrow.

It was a long wait - an exercise in patience, which the gerbil won! These desert rodents are so shy that it is difficult to get a good look at them in the wild, even though their tracks can be seen often. It is said that they like to eat the seeds of the desert squash, which other animals shun. There certainly were enough of these yellow tennis balls lying around to provide a feast for many gerbils.

A little bit further on we came upon an entirely different kind of ball - this one was the size of a large pomelo and bristled with black spines: a hedgehog out on an early evening stroll. We lifted him gingerly and found he was surprisingly heavy for his size. Not a single part of his body was unprotected by his sharp spines. We put him down on a large patch of sand and sat down to wait again. This time it did not take long before the creature relaxed and poked out a pointed, black nose. Now it was possible to identify him: an Ethiopian hedgehog, one of the two species

The Ethiopian hedgehog has a black face.

of this desert area. He looked left and right, decided it was safe, and showed the rest of his face. A large black tick was fastened to his forehead, looking like a third eye! Suddenly his legs appeared and he ran off at a fast trot as I followed him with my camera. He looked quite funny, and it took me a minute before I realised why. Most small animals walk on their toes; this little guy had large flat feet, like Charlie Chaplin's boots.

A third nocturnal animal occurs here, but so far we have never seen one alive and well. The Caracal Lynx is so shy and swift, it is extremely difficult to observe. Recently one was found on the Dubai/Al Ain road, unfortunately a victim of a speeding car.

Rarely, Gordon's wildcat is seen by overnight campers. But even if you see it, you may not recognise it for the rarity it is. It is a lovely small cat, with a broad face and large ears and a bushy black-tipped tail. Few still occur in the wild, and their continued existence is threatened, both by inter-breeding with domestic cats, and by the destruction of their desert habitat.

The lovely Gordon's wildcat is threatened with extinction.

Moths

CC found a large moth on a wall and gave it to me to photograph. It was a very strange insect with a wing-span of 8 cm or more - surely one of the largest moths I have seen. When we picked it up to position it on a piece of rock, it emitted a loud, whirring sound - obviously a distress signal. But it sat quietly -it is a nocturnal animal and this was midday. Its velvety upper wings had brown and black markings and underneath the lower wings were a rich ochre yellow. The body was a lighter yellow with grey-blue stripes. But the most remarkable feature was a hump on its thorax, marked with a pale oval patch in the shape of a human skull. Large black eyes and quivering striped antennae adorned the rather small head. This Death Head hawk moth (*Acherontia atropos*) is quite prevalent in the UAE and according to the ENHG records, its caterpillar feeds on the evergreen bushes of the verbenaceae as well as on petunias and members of the Nightshade family. Often the adults are found around beehives, where they steal honey as an easy source of energy - easy, but not safe, since the bees may kill them and often do. Later, I read that the Death Head hawk moth occurs in practically every country in the world. The

A Striped hawk moth is quite small.

The large moths: The Oleander hawk moth and the Death Head hawk moth.

Hawk moth caterpillars have horns at their rear ends.

sound they make is similar to sounds that bees make to one another when they want to communicate that everything is OK in the hive - a very clever ruse of the moth to avoid being attacked by the bees.

The other large moth that I have seen is the Oleander hawk moth *(Daphnis retii)*, whose caterpillar - not unsurprisingly - feeds on oleander bushes. I like it even better. Its markings are in camouflage pattern of orangey-pink, olive green and variety of browns. It lays its 2 mm eggs on the underside of a leaf near the top of an oleander bush. The small caterpillar is reportedly pale yellow with a black abdominal horn and as it grows older it turns green with a yellow horn, with two large blue "eyes" on the side of the body behind the head. Just before pupation it turns dark brown.

Other hawk moths, which have been sighted by members of the Natural History Group, are the Hummingbird hawk moth *(Macroglossum stellatatum)*, with a wing-span of 3.5 cm; the somewhat larger Striped hawk moth *(Hyles livornica)* 6 cm wing-span and the very large Silver striped hawk moth *(Hippotion celerio)* 7 to 8 cm wing-span. Of these, the first is a day-flying moth that hovers in front of flowers as it projects its proboscis inside to drink.

Wildlife around the house

For a few months I lived in an apartment building that also housed numerous pigeons. One day we had visitors. Two birds flew up to the holes in the concrete lace work at the sides of the balcony, screeching like ordinary crows. They feigned attacks, made more impressive by their blood-curdling shrieks, but the pigeons did not budge. The birds finally flew off to a tree across the road and settled in the top.

I observed them through the binoculars, and decided they were Common Mynahs, of which the *Birds of Oman* book gives a good description. I recalled that mynahs have a wide range of melodious songs, but the sound display that they had just put on was far from melodious. However, a minute later they burst into song, and you could hardly believe that they were the same creatures that had tried to chase the pigeons out of the coveted nesting places.

The mynahs are not indigenous to this area, but have probably been brought from the Indian subcontinent, as happened with the Ring-necked Parakeets that you can see flying from Jumeirah towards Deira just before sunset every evening.

These birds are an extremely hardy species, having managed to survive in both temperate and tropical climates. Colonies in UAE cities are increasing in size continuously. I enjoy watching their antics in the evening sky, with the sun glowing on their long green and turquoise tail feathers.

I once had the opportunity to observe one in captivity. She amazed me with her repertoire of sounds: apart from the raucous screams and ear-splitting shrieks, she could do a perfect cat-call. She had melodious whistles, pleading whines, whispers, clicks, tut-tuts, and creaks, and sometimes even a six-note song. I was intrigued by the agility of her big beak and fleshy tongue. She could crack a water melon seed and extract the thin sliver from the centre without dropping any of the pieces. She was crazy about fruit and I wondered what fruits the feral birds can find here, apart from dates. Another, as yet unanswered, question is: where do these parakeets nest? They usually need hollow spaces in high trees or buildings. Do they use the Deira wind-towers? Or have they adapted to this environment with its lack of high hollow trees by choosing an entirely different kind of nesting site?

A Ring-necked Parakeet showing off its beautiful colours.

Common mynahs on camel back (Photo: M West).

Chapter 5

SEPTEMBER

OCTOBER

It is still hot but the temperatures are steadily falling, making conditions more pleasant all the time. With the days still long, the late afternoon is a good time to go out, temperatures having dropped to around 28°C by nightfall.

Birdwatchers are privileged people in these months. The UAE lies at the crossroads of two major migration routes from Europe to Asia and Africa. The increased size of plantations and insect populations, and the availability of water here, have made this area a favourite stopover for the birds - in fact, a number of species spend all winter here and are even starting to breed in the Emirates.

The best places to observe birds are Dubai Creek, Safa and Mushrif Parks in Dubai, the Al Ain Zoo, the Jebel Ali Hotel grounds, the mangrove marshes of Kalba and Abu Dhabi, and the sewage plant area of Abu Dhabi.

Abool

We drove past Fossil Valley to Mahdah, and skirted the large oasis on the new macadam road till we reached the fort. There we turned on to a dirt track that crossed the flat plain between Jebel Hawrah and the Hajar mountains. We discussed whether this was a wide wadi or an alluvial plain - it was hard to tell. The track became rough. We then forded a stream in which calcium-rich pools sparkled turquoise and white between the reeds and sedges. The mountains closed in on us and at the mouth of a valley stood a fort.

This was really a fortified house which was occupied up to 15 years ago. Remnants of walls, forming squares and rectangles on the hills surrounding the big house, might have been part of the fortifications. Here and there pulicaria and ochradenus bushes still bloomed with yellow flowers, and a few samr trees provided shade.

The fort itself had a small courtyard with large, carved wooden doors. We entered through a much smaller, rounded gate, which was set into one of the larger doors. To our left was a tower; on two other sides of the courtyard were several rooms and a smaller tower. Many slanted shooting holes were set in the thick walls, commanding every area of the valley. The lintel over one of the entrances was made of intricately carved wood, held in place by woven ropes.

Old door in Abool fort.

Between the stark rocks one can find cool pools.

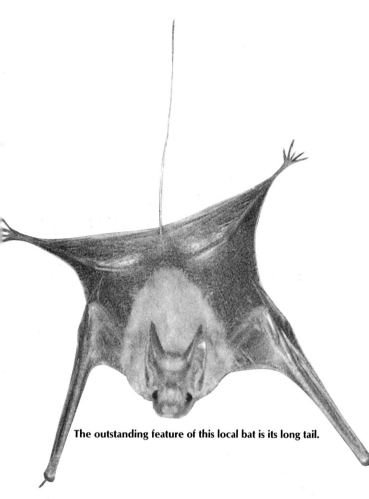

The outstanding feature of this local bat is its long tail.

Golden-eyed toad peeps from its hide. There are no frogs in Arabia.

When we entered the high tower, half a dozen bats flew out of the windows and up into the stairwell. One was in such a hurry that it hit one of our group square on the cheek.

"And I always thought they were equipped with radar," grumbled the victim. "They are not supposed to crash into things, let alone people!" Some bats had not panicked, and remained hanging upside down from the rafters in the tower. Their beady eyes looked intently down their pointed noses. They held their wings spread wide and a mousy tail stuck up straight between their hind legs.

Outside the breeze blew hot air from the valley as we continued on our way to an old village which lay overlooking a large and luscious oasis.

We descended to the level of the wadi and crossed it to enter the shade of the palms and fruit trees. A large, blue-flowering bush was host to a couple of beautifully patterned swallowtail butterflies. A huge mango tree dwarfed the other trees in the nakheel, and lime trees were abundant. One kind of citrus tree bore large fruit which I recognised as pomelos. The weight of the grapefruit-sized fruits pulled the branches of the tree all the way down to the ground. A pomegranate tree was decorated with dark red globes of half ripe fruits.

The silence of the morning was punctuated by the sweet call of the bulbuls, but they did not show themselves readily. Underneath a lemon tree a large stand of jasmin showed its sweet-smelling, perfectly white flowers.

A new concrete falaj had been constructed, robbing the old mud one of whatever water there was - there was little anyway. For the plants which we were trying to find this was bad news. A concrete falaj does not leak water to the surrounding earth, and, consequently, the habitat of the orchids and lilies that used to grow here was being destroyed. Still, we searched, following both the old and the new falaj. They led to a crystal-clear pond, bordered with maidenhair ferns, *Bacopa monnieri* and *Lippia nodiflora* plants. Of the lilies we saw no sign, but many orchid plants showed new shoots, as yet without flowers. To my joy I found a *Centaurium pulchellum* plant with its pink flower wide open.

On a fallow field between a number of purple-flowering vernonia plants, we found a Wolf spider prowling about. Its eight red eyes glittered on its forehead, as the hairy legs parted the blades of grass. This is a species of spider that does not make a web, but hunts actively for its prey. It was well camouflaged in the dry brownish grass, and we tried to manoeuvre it to a spot where it could be photographed.

Beyond Dqaiq

We turned off the Sohar road towards the area of our favourite wadi and found that a new road had been constructed. A smooth sandy ribbon billowed up and down the hills in front of us. Taken at speed, it was as exhilarating as being on a roller coaster. Two villages and their beautiful oases were bypassed completely, a fact undoubtedly enjoyed by the villagers who can now have peaceful Fridays!

The road took us far beyond the point which, up till then, we had been able to reach on foot only.

We stopped at a part of the wadi that looked interesting. I had some misgivings about the heat of early September, but, when we alighted from the car, it was surprisingly pleasant, with a cool breeze softening the impact of the sun's rays. The water level in the wadi was much lower than before, but there were still several pools deep enough for swimming.

The vegetation was sparse. Of all the plants which I had seen here in the winter, only a few palms and oleanders remained, with here and there a dry clump of incense grass. We reached a deep pool and stopped to bathe. The water was like soft cool silk and as we floated in the shallows, small fish nibbled at our feet and fingers. My friends wanted to explore farther, but I decided to stay behind.

As had happened so often before, as soon as I was alone and quiet, the area around me became more alive. Instead of a few brave fish, dozens emerged. Little beetles scurried to and fro on the surface of the water. One was the backswimmer, a small insect with paddle-like hind legs, who rests upside down beneath the surface of the water. It is kept afloat by a bubble of air, which it carries pressed to its abdomen as a supply of oxygen. Several empty skins of dragonfly larvae floated by. Two wasps with orange-brown bodies and yellow markings on the abdomen hovered nearby. They were obviously attracted to my red toenails. I put my feet in the water, preferring a soft fish nibble to a possible sting. My friendly neighbourhood entomologist later identified the insects as *Vespa orientalis,* a local wasp, which does,

A well camouflaged Wolf-spider on the prowl.

Vespa orientalis seems attracted to red colours.

in fact, sting (though only the female, of course). They are not aggressive, unless their nests are disturbed.

Suddenly a deafening clap of thunder shattered the silence. I nearly fell off my rock with surprise. The sky above me was still blue, and nothing indicated a change in the weather. But over the eastern slope behind me a huge black cloud had formed. Lightning ripped the clouds apart and a strong gust of wind howled through the canyon where I sat. I hoped my friends would return quickly, for I had heard of the dangers of flash floods and I did not care to be caught in one. Neither did my friends, apparently, for they came running back, jumping from rock to rock. We got back to the car in time to see that the cloudburst had taken place in the next valley. A fresh smell of water-soaked sand and cooled rock hung in the air. Small streams came rushing down in the gutters, overflowing on to the road, taking big chunks out of the embankment.

A bit further along a four-metre wide stream crossed the road to form a huge waterfall on the far side - a sheet of water rushing straight down over several metres.

A local girl was looking out across the water and when she saw us, she shook her head in wonder and said "A lot of water today!"

We forded the stream, feeling quite adventurous and were awarded with a fabulous view from the next hilltop. The sound of rushing water filled the air and several small waterfalls could be seen in the distance. But then we reached an area where some real damage had been done. The road had been completely washed away. Wild water cascaded over the rocks at the bottom of a two-metre deep canyon, carrying debris, mud and parts of oleander bushes. There was no way to get across the three-metre-wide gap, so we just sat and watched the spectacle for a while.

I was amazed to see, from traces of debris on the sides of the wadi, that the water must at one time have reached a height of three metres above the level of the road. A solid wall of water must have come rushing down. Awed by the power that was revealed, I decided to take the dangers of flash floods even more seriously in future.

Jebel Hafeet

Standing on a vast plain underneath a blue sky littered with high cumulus clouds, with a stiff breeze tearing at my jacket, I could imagine myself in my native Holland, except for the range of golden-brown mountains that stretched along the horizon.

We were spending an afternoon exploring the alluvial plain between Jebel Hafeet and the Hajar mountains. I wanted to see the cairns dating from the third millenium BC that are located on the east side of the Bare Mountain.

Our view towards the foothills from the road was hampered by a miles-long man-made dyke that stretched all the way from Mazyad to the northern tip of the mountain, so we had parked the car and were walking across the plain to investigate.

I saw a scurrying movement in a small clump of *Hammada elegans.* It was a beautiful beetle, the size of a prune-pip, matt black with a design of white spots on its back that made it look like a sunflower seed. A second one peeped out from behind some stems and obligingly stayed in view to be photographed. We coaxed it from between the branches to get it into the sunlight for better observation. It scuttled away across the sand and then suddenly stopped, half raised its body and sat motionless on its

"Sunflower-seed" beetle.

hind legs for quite a while. Was that a sanitary stop or what? We crouched down to watch.

"Look, it is laying eggs - do you see that tiny tube extending from her belly into the sand?"

The beetle had just finished and had started to scratch grains of sand over the spot where she had been sitting. She ran off again to repeat the process a few centimetres further on. This time, the camera was ready for the happening and the magnifying lens showed clearly that our beetle was busy ensuring the continuation of her species.

From the sky the croak of a raven could be heard. CC looked up to see a falcon swooping down on the bird. The raven rolled over, his claws stretched out defensively, then fell away in a perfect roll and escaped.

The Bare Mountain lay huge and forbidding in front of us, seemingly desolate, devoid of life - but small scenes of imminent birth and death, such as we had witnessed, were taking place all around it.

Climbing Jebel Hafeet

Jebel Hafeet lies like a beached whale at the south-eastern tip of Al Ain. We had decided on a two-pronged attack; two of us climbing the south-west slope to the summit and the other two traversing along the top to meet there. Traversing the top sounded easier, so I was one of the two who left their car at the end of the road that was being constructed at the northern end. The road ended at a deep abyss that split the mountain across its full width. This we had to cross, by climbing down one steep slope and up the other side. I was grateful for sturdy mountain shoes, but found out soon that I could have used some gloves as well. The weathered limestone rock was sharp and there was never a spot level enough to stand unsupported. When I reached the bottom and looked back I wondered how I ever got down - and worse, how I'd ever get back up.

One advantage of scrambling up a steep mountain side is that your nose is always only inches away from the ground and that way you can hardly miss the small plants that grow between the rocks. I was delighted to find a minute plant with orange and red paper-like flowers - or fruit wings, as I found out later. These "flowers" of *Salsola rubescens* resemble those of the *Hammada elegans,* that grows abundantly at lower altitudes, but the leaves are quite different and the colours are more pronounced.

After the first cleft, a second, smaller one followed, and when we had crossed that, we emerged on to a high plateau that afforded a grand view over the red sand dunes of the north-eastern tip of the Empty Quarter. Towards the north the ponds of Ayn Al Faydah bounced back the sunlight like mirrors. Al Ain, beyond, was lost in dust and heat haze.

We walked across the plateau and saw a wide wadi opening up in front of us. It came down in zigzags from the summit and curved westward to a break in the mountainside, some 50 metres or more below our feet. The slope down was an easy scramble over loose scree and at the bottom there was a surprising amount of greenery. The wadi bed was dry, but huge, smooth rock pools had been carved out by the circular motion of boulders swept along in wild currents.

What a fantastic sight this wadi must be after heavy rain! Some rocks were shaped into bizarre forms: skulls, dragons, owl faces - it was like a gallery of surrealistic art. In between the sculptures grew stands of reeds, oleander and several kinds of grasses.

We followed the gentle slope of the wadi as it meandered up to the summit. At one curve so many bushes grew, it seemed like a garden. A member of the rock rose family *Helianthemum kahiricum,* put forth its yellow flowers with the petals characteristically folded backwards to reveal the crown of stamens and pistil.

The course of the wadi had become so steep again that we were back to hand-over-hand climbing, and, after a while, I gave up and stopped in the shade of a lonely sidr tree, while my companion carried on towards the summit.

After some refreshment I slowly walked back down the wadi and up the scree slope again and settled on the high rock plateau to wait for the others.

A few metres below me a Rock Thrush was singing, the fragile notes of its song contrasting sweetly with the harsh immensity of its surroundings. The bird flew closer and sat down at a metre's distance. It did not seem interested in the breadcrumbs which I tossed its way. Instead, it fluttered up and came straight for my head. Instinctively, I ducked, and, in doing so, scared it off - but I'll never stop wondering whether it would really have sat down on my head if I'd kept still...

Jebel Qatar

When we set out to climb the lowest of the three mountains around Al Ain, it was still cool. The light was clear, and from the road, we could see the steep cliff of Jebel Qatar rising up from the plain. The wadi, which we followed on foot, after having parked the cars, had little water but plenty of greenery, and was brightly lit by the early sunlight. We rounded a bend and were confronted with an enormous petrified waterfall - at least, that is what it looked like. Huge stone steps and terraces had been cut out of the mountain side by prehistoric torrential floods. A stand of palm trees at the bottom was dwarfed by the massive wall.

We started to pick our way up the steps, which turned out to be no easy matter. The stones were polished smooth and offered us no hand or footholds. But in the end we all reached the top, where a panoramic view unfolded. On the gravel plain

giant. Above us towered 50 metres or more of vertical rock-face, seemingly impregnable. We followed the base of the cliff northwards for another hundred metres. This part was shaded and it was so pleasant there, with a view so spectacular, that I decided to remain behind and let the others proceed with their athletic efforts.

Soon the noise of their voices and the clatter of their boots died away, and the more subtle sounds of nature became audible.

A busy insect droned in the midday heat, and a pair of delicate white and yellow butterflies fluttered around the tiny trumpets of a desert thorn *(Lycium shawii)*. A lizard slithered away behind some rocks before I could identify it.

A huge tree grew perpendicular to the rock face and its almost horizontal trunk offered a wonderful seat. I settled down among the leaves with a large branch as a backrest and listened to the serendipitous bird-song that tumbled down the mountainside to the plain below.

Jebel Qatar at dawn.

below, subterraneous water courses were outlined by the presence of ghaf trees and shrubs. Far away on the horizon, were the red sand dunes along the Al Ain-Dubai road. Bizarre-shaped rocks were tumbled together to form dark caves and tunnels. In between grew large bushes of *Capparis cartilaginea*, a member of the Caper family.

Even by mid-morning the heat was already turning the white flowers to shades ranging from pink to dark red. You have to be an early bird to see these flowers in their full glory.

After having traversed a relatively easy slope, we had to scramble again across huge slabs of aggregated rock that looked as if they had been tossed down from the high cliffs by some bad-tempered

The vastness of the view and the silence, accented by these joyous sounds, were overwhelming. I could not get enough of it. I was absorbing it as if my soul craved it, like a thirsty man craves water.

A bird flew along the cliffs, and as it passed my tree, it caught sight of me. Its immediate reaction to this unusual, large "flower" was quite amusing. It stopped flying forward and instead fluttered up and down several times to get a good look. Then it circled around and landed on a rock nearby. It hopped closer and turned its head this way and that to observe me from all possible angles. So we sat, regarding each other seriously, until the bird decided that I was harmless and uninteresting, and swept down into the valley again.

On another occasion we explored the southern cliffs of the Jebel. A dry wadi leads up to a place which I have named the "Hanging gardens of Babylon".

There were many large trees with abundant green foliage around: samr, sidr, ghaf, wild fig and oleander. Between smooth rocks a few stagnant pools covered with algae provided enough moisture for stands of *Phragmites australis, Tephrosia apollinea* and several grasses.

We started to climb the first waterfall, which was dry. At the point where the boulders became too huge for me to negotiate, I climbed up the side, a steep slope made dangerous because of loose stones and brittle rocks. A luxuriant green tree, which I had never seen before, cast its shadow on the slope. Its branches ended in clusters of tiny blossoms and berries which varied in colour from pale yellow to pink to dark red and purple. It was *Salvadora persica*, the toothbrush tree, of which a cultivated variety lines the Al Ain roads. Higher up I saw a lone shrub, which looked like *Moringa peregrina*, but this was the first one I had ever seen at this altitude and in this area.

One of our group called me over to inspect a curious plant. It consisted of two or three tightly closed woody buds, growing close to the ground, with one tap-root about eight to 10 cms in length. There were many of these plants around, so I picked a couple.

As we sat down for a snack and a drink, I accidentally spilled some water on the specimens. A few seconds later the tight buds started to unfold and within minutes I held a cluster of little "flowers" - five woody petals and five larger sepals surrounding a heart of dried seeds. The speed with which this process took place was amazing. I like the name of this plant: *Asteriscus pygmaeus* - dwarf star!

There is another plant which shows similar hygroscopic properties, and it also grows here: *Anastatica hierochuntica* or the rose of Jericho. But this plant, which in its dried-up state looks like a tightly clenched fist, takes much longer to unfold when immersed in water. During heavy rainfalls, the plants will unfold and disperse the seeds, which then grow a rosette of leaves with a cluster of central pale blue flowers.

I wandered off to where a lot of greenery peeked between boulders as large as houses.

A large, dry pool lay at the foot of an equally dry

This hanging vine (Cocculus hirsutus) must be very old to have grown to this size.

Asteriscus pygmaeus seedpods unfold when doused with water.

The pool at Khudayrah has become a popular tourist spot.

waterfall. The apparent lack of water had not inhibited the growth of my hanging gardens however. The yellow-pink cliffs were cracked in a criss-cross pattern, so that it looked as if the entire wall had been put together of children's playing blocks. Between the cracks, plants had found footholds. High up there was a wild fig tree, then a dark bush, that looked like *Hammada elegans,* and beside it a veil of light green foliage that reached a length of some 15 metres. Its free-hanging branches swung lightly in the breeze.

The shiny leaves and white flowers of another capparis plant formed a counterpoint to the left. Lower down another wild fig stood between dusty grey *Dyerophytum indicum* trees with their sprays of inconspicuous orange flowers. Around the pool some annuals were growing. Dark green thistle leaves with white veins grew in decorative rosettes between dozens of small stingless nettles. CC climbed up to the huge hanging vine to get me a specimen. He practically disappeared against the background of awesome rocks. The vine originated from a large, woody stem and was obviously extremely old. It turned out to be called *Cocculus hirsutus.*

To the right of the waterfall a strange geological configuration had been formed by many years of dripping of water that contained some kind of mineral. A bizarre sienna-coloured rock towered over smaller, grey shapes, which looked like lace.

As I gazed at this wonderful place, there was a sudden movement in the foliage. A large bird swooped down, heading for a group of noisy pigeons on the other side of the valley. They scattered in all directions, and though the attacker made another desultory pass at them, he did not catch anything. Instead, he soared up and circled with widespread motionless wings above me. His large wingspan, the small head and the white markings on his overall brown wings made him out to be, most probably, a Tawny Eagle.

Khudayrah

A day off in the middle of the week always gives me a special sense of freedom - so this Sunday morning looked extra bright as we clambered down the steep bank to the swimming hole at Wadi Khudayrah.

The pool lay like a grey-green mirror between the cliffs. The silence was interrupted by the soft gurgle of water on the pebbles and the sweet song of an invisible bird overhead.

My friends were hesitant to follow me in my swim upstream to the waterfall, so I had the place to myself. Where the gorge narrowed, the rocks had been cut into wonderful shapes, rising up on either side to a height of some eight metres. In some parts the sky was obscured by the bulging outcrops, but here and there the sunlight reached down and turned the water a golden-flecked emerald green.

I floated quietly around a corner and then stared in wonder: in the middle of the stream a rock jutted out above the level of the water, and on top perched a kingfisher. He was like a piece of brilliant jewellery with the sunlight striking his blue and green feathers. He looked at me over his shoulder for a long moment before flying up and away into the canyon. I had seen him there before, but only as a quick flash of colour among the rocks. An eye-to-eye encounter like this was rare and lovely.

Hatta

The October hike of the Natural History Group was supposed to be a botanical trip, but the rains had been too recent for the annuals to have come out or the perennials to have flowered. The rocky plain that is the wide part of Wadi Khabb still looked barren and brown, with little colour.

A stand of *Euphorbia larica* was flowering, and I pointed out the shiny greenish-yellow flowers to the group members. The euphorbias, of which there are many different species in the UAE, have adapted in different ways to different circumstances.

In shady and humid oases you find plants with large leaves and fragile thin stems, whereas, out on this hot plain, the euphorbia we were looking at seemed to consist only of light green bare branches. In fact, these are the leaves which have reduced their surface area to the smallest size possible, and are growing in such a way (straight up towards the sky) that only a few millimetres of surface are hit by direct sunlight. The flowers too are small, clinging close to the stems, and they have thick, succulent petals, that are covered with a waxy layer that reflects the sunlight. Everything is aimed at conserving moisture and preventing dehydration.

Recently I saw a picture in a book about the flora of Yemen of yet another euphorbia, which I would have taken for a cactus, had I not known that cacti occur *only* on the American continent (in the wild, at least). The leaves of this euphorbia had become globular, containing a large amount of water, and the surface was ribbed and studded with spines. The air between the ribs and spines retains moisture more easily, and the pores through which the plant breathes are hidden in the recesses, thus again reducing the chance of dehydration. It was amazing to see that the euphorbia of the Arabian peninsula and the cactus of the American continent had both adapted to similar climates in a way that gave them a similar appearance. The principle is called *convergence,* and it occurs in animals as well as plants.

A bit further along I found a flowering specimen of the eyelash plant *Blepharis ciliaris.* Its pale blue, one-petalled flower curved up gracefully between the grey-green spiky leaves. This plant has an unique device for propagating itself. When the dried-up plant is inundated during a rain-shower a hygroscopic mechanism is triggered that shoots the seeds in all directions over distances of six to ten feet. It looks like a machine-gun nest in action. I have only seen it in a movie, so far, since I have never been around an eyelash plant during a heavy rain.

Excited cries were coming from a group of people near a rock. A Blue-headed agama in full colour was perched there, fearlessly glaring at the crowd that surrounded him. He was a beautiful deep blue, which may have been even more pronounced by our vexing presence. But he posed willingly enough and then ambled off to higher grounds. Some people followed him and had the good luck to see him catch a bright red dragonfly!!

A delicate butterfly was disturbed and flew away to settle on a rock close by my feet. I had never seen one like this before. It was dark blue with black, outlined in velvety grey.

Then another flash of blue caught my eye-this time way up in the sky. An Indian Roller was heading north towards the lush, insect-infested gardens of the Hatta Fort Hotel.

I caught up with a few fellow-hikers and asked: "Did you see that Blue-headed agama?"

"No," was the reply. "But we have a lizard here with a turquoise tail!"

That was exciting. Could it be a Blue-tailed skink? It was clinging to the rocks in the shade of an overhang, which was most unskink-like behaviour. It had a slender body of about 12 cms long, and its tail

The Giant Waterbug hunts in the streams.

was at least twice that and brilliant turquoise, which appeared even more flashy when it ran out of its hiding place into the sunlight.

The sun was beaming down and the sparkling water that rushed through the rock crevices looked inviting. The water was cold and refreshing - in fact, after a while, it felt positively good to be in the hot sun again.

I sat on a ledge with my feet still in the stream, watching a brown leaf float downstream.

"That is a large leaf", I thought - and then realised that leaves of such size and shape could not occur in this area. Moreover, a leaf with two large claws and two pairs of legs could not occur anywhere at all! It was a nice specimen of the Giant Waterbug, a common but interesting insect of the wadis. They are excellent swimmers and fliers, and they can fly off to wetter parts if their pond runs dry. In close-up, the insect was quite attractive. Its back was adorned with a pattern of interlacing rhomboids in various shades of brown. Its head had light yellow stripes and a pug "nose" between two large shiny eyes.

For quite a while I have confused these Giant Waterbugs with Water Scorpions, which are also common. The latter is a smaller, more slender insect, and is not as nicely marked. The main distinguishing feature is a long tube (actually consisting of two separate half-tubes) extending from the end of its abdomen. This is a breathing tube, which the insect pushes up through the surface of the water.

The Giant Waterbug, on the other hand, breathes by way of an air-bubble, which it holds in the space between its wings and its body. It has to surface every 30 to 60 minutes to get a fresh supply of air.

Even though our trip had not been a botanical success, we had ample opportunity to observe some interesting bits of nature in the desert...

A small "Blue" resting.

Bird-watching

Being quite short-sighted I am not much of a bird-watcher. The parks in Dubai are such marvellous places to study birds, however, that even I am starting to recognise a few species. Quite a few are easily observed from the car. Frequently, Crested Larks can be seen by the roadside, while wagtails and mynahs tend to hop around on roundabouts and road-dividers. Indian Rollers sit on telephone wires or lamp-posts, and the Palm Doves are with us everywhere.

A visit to Safa Park during the autumn migration was memorable. The first bird we saw was a small, light grey one, slender, with a long tail and delicate legs. It hopped up and down the stem of a palm tree, tearing off fibres in search of little creepy-crawlies, a Graceful Warbler.

Easier to spot was the Hoopoe. This attractive bird has black and white checkered wings and long crest feathers with the same pattern. It hopped around on the grass, poking its long curved beak into the lawn, in search of termites and ants. To my delight, it cocked its headgear once, displaying its full glory.

As we left the sidewalk to cross over to the irrigation pond, a cluster of crimson-flowered plants caught my attention. I recognised it as a salt-tolerant succulent, *Sesuvium verrucosum*. The crimson flowers, with their many white stamens, are tucked between dark green thick leaves and sturdy stems.

We reached the edge of the pool - a still, black water reflecting the myriad hues of green from the surrounding trees and bushes. One patch of green detached itself from a branch and skitted across to the other side with a familiar raucous scream - a Ring-necked Parakeet! Then, one after the other, two large birds unfolded powder blue wings marked with indigo and disappeared quietly into more distant shrubbery. They were European Rollers, slightly different from their relatives, the Indian Rollers.

By this time we had met up with some bird experts from the Natural History Group.

"Did you see that Golden Oriole that flew over your head just now?" someone aked.

"Oh no, we missed it!" We were disappointed. CC had not seen an oriole in over thirty years and I had never seen one at all, since they were already rare in Holland when I lived there as a teenager.

Our friends reassured us: "Don't worry, there are quite a few around now. In fact there is a female sitting right across from us in that tree".

Once it was pointed out to us, the shape of the bird was clear, but its colour was camouflaged by the shaded greenery in which it was hiding.

A grey Night Heron flapped across the water and a small teal swam from behind a fallen tree. Across the meadow I watched another European Roller, then suddenly I saw a yellow bird settle in a casuarina tree nearby.

"Look, an oriole!" The bird obliged by glidding across an open space to the next tree, but then it hid stubbornly and the half second glimpse was all we were allowed to see of this lovely bird.

High up in the sky a chirping call was repeated from many directions.

"Bee-eaters", said the experts.

But where were they? We strained to see, and presently we could make out a few black dots flitting across our field of vision. We tried to count them - half a dozen, 10, 20, even 30. They came closer and closer, swooping down from great heights (they can fly to 25,000 feet, I was told!!) down to where we

Sesuvium verrucosum is a coastal succulent.

were. Then they were all around us, skimming the water at incredible speed. The copper-red and yellow of their backs and faces flashed in the sunshine, and when they turned their bellies up in a curve, they showed shades of brown and green. Like a handful of jewellery they tumbled around us, zipping and diving in astounding aerobatics. Their shapes were reflected in the black mirror of the pool, as they zeroed in on the insects that had been enjoying a peaceful morning up till now.

Even the experts were amazed. This was as good a display of European Bee-eaters as they had ever seen here. As suddenly as the birds had appeared they were gone. But we could still hear their trilling call as they rested, out of sight in some high trees.

Returning back in the shade of the mesquite trees, we saw another European friend, a cuckoo. He was also spotted by some house-crows in the neighbouring trees. They dropped from the trees with excited croaks, and it was quite a while before they settled down again. The sudden appearance of the cuckoo had scared them because he resembles a kestrel both in shape and flight pattern.

Flocks of European Bee-eaters visit the UAE twice a year (Photo: M West).

Chapter 6

NOVEMBER
DECEMBER

It is cooler now, but not yet the best time to enjoy to the full desert plant life. The seeds of last season lie waiting for rain, but more than just a simple shower is needed for these seeds to germinate. Only when they are soaked for a prolonged time does the protective covering of the seeds dissolve, thus allowing the plant to grow. In a dry year, few annuals will be around. But the perennial plants are rapidly recovering from the effect of the blistering heat and new sprouts and buds can be found on many of them.

One common saltbush in the Emirates, *Hammada elegans*, is at its best in December — not because it is in bloom, however. Along the roads to Hatta and Al Ain one can see dozens of these bushes covered with transparent white, pink and purplish fruit-wings.

Sharm

We drove downstream in the dry wadi towards the fort at Sharm. On the left, where the falaj was located, green palms hugged the steep bank. To the right, the orange-red hills were bare rock, except for those areas where some hidden water had caused small rock gardens to grow with a variety of shrubs and weeds.

At the point where a rocky outcrop jutted into the wadi, the fort could be seen, rising high above the surrounding greenery. It has long since been deserted and is slowly falling to pieces. The village behind it has also been deserted, but the lush palm groves at the foot of the hill are still being used.

The small oasis is one of my favourite haunts, since there are so many wild plants and insects among the date palms. Walking uphill, we crossed the falaj, which is cemented neatly, but does not look as attractive as the mudbanked ones elsewhere. A thicket on the right I knew to be mulberry trees, which have - in season - black and red berries among the light green leaves. Just behind it, a sweet-smelling mimosa tree lifted joyous yellow branches towards the blue sky.

I clambered over a small wall and edged behind some sharp-leaved palms. Between the grass that grew there on the small plots, I saw several flowering weeds. One looked similar in colour and shape to autumn asters - bright purple composite flowers on high stems - an odd colour to find here. Another had

Mulberries grow in the oases.

reddish green buds like small berries right on the stem between the leaves. Both plants were new to me and were later identified as a *Vernonia arabica* and *Euphorbia hirta,* respectively.

On a large bush of *Withania somnifera* which had green flowers and brilliant red berries, I saw a strange beetle: it had a squarish carapace with a triangular head and hind legs, which had bulging "thighs". The creature was a stinkbug, one of many species found in the area.

On close inspection it turned out that only one of each pair (the male?) had the "thighs". The bush was infested with the bugs, who were so busy mating that they were not disturbed at all by my taking close-up pictures of them.

A flash of vermillion red caught my eye - it was the flower of a pomegranate. On the same bush, the beginning of the fruit had its orange fruit-wings spread out to look like yet another flower.

Close to the fort a second species of acacia was in flower. Its globular flowers were almost white and much larger than those of the tree at the entrance of the grove. I touched the fluffy softness of the flowers with my nose, but there was no scent. Quite a few of the 700 different species of acacia which exist in the world occur in the Emirates and I have not figured out yet which is which. As long as there remains so much to find out, I'll never have a dull moment.

Hatta

To our left the hills rose higher and higher to where the majestic mountains shimmered blue in the sun. To our right, beyond the deep canyon of the wadi, was a scene that resembled a moonscape, forbidding in its apparently lifeless bleakness. But, from previous trips, I knew that even the bleakest hill or valley harbours plants, sometimes even in flower, and many species of animals. On a previous occasion I had seen a fox here, which, surprised by my appearance on a hilltop, fled at great speed into the valley beyond.

CC pointed out a small funnel in the sand at my feet: "Do you know what that is?"

I remembered vaguely that it was a kind of trap to catch insects, but I had to be reminded of the name of the hunter: the antlion. This ferociously-named creature is actually the larva of a winged insect. As a larva, it lives on smaller insects which it catches in a

Stinkbugs secrete a malodorous fluid when touched.

The Jewel beetle feeds on Acacia tortilis.

Orchids and ferns in a desert area!

The small pits are insect traps of a tiny predator: the antlion (2 mm).

A velvety-grey and gold bug.

funnel-shaped hole that it digs in the sand. It sits at the bottom of its trap and waits until tell-tale grains of sand, disturbed by the presence of a small insect, drop down. Then - believe it or not - it bombards its prey with grains of sand, so that it looses its balance on the sloping surface of the funnel and comes tumbling down to the bottom, where the antlion waits to devour it.

Close to the numerous funnels we saw the smallest of scorpions - a little creature, barely four mms long, with microscopic pincers sticking out defiantly in front.

"Let's throw it to the lions".

We manoeuvred it on to the loose sand of a funnel, and suddenly there was a quick movement and the scorpion was gone. At the bottom of the funnel we could see a number of tiny legs engaged in a fierce fight to the death. It lasted for seconds only, then there was a small pause... and the scorpion emerged victorious. It went its way, seemingly undisturbed by the disruption of its routine.

I laughed, thinking of cock-fights, bull-fights and heavyweight fights in the Bronx. None on this tiny scale, yet all so similar nonetheless! I imagined cheering crowds of ants and sandflies, but there was no sound in the silence of the plain and the hills.

The walk along the bottom of the wide, dry wadi was a pleasant one now. A cool breeze took the sting out of the sun's rays and the high walls surrounding us did not yet radiate heat as they do in the summer. Those banks of the wadi - sometimes over 20 metres high - are a miracle in themselves.

There must have been a lot more water at one time to create this wadi. Now there was none. The small streams and pools that I had visited some time earlier had all dried up. Where did the fish and the toads go? Are they still there, hidden in cool, wet gravel underneath the overhanging rocks? And if they died, how is it that they always reappear when the water returns? I knew that this particular wadi still had lots of flowing water a few kilometers upstream, but some of the smaller streams dry up completely during droughts, and yet life always reappears with the rains.

I saw a small butterfly on a tephrosia bush and sat down close by to observe and photograph it. On top its wings were a delicate shade of blue, but I could only catch short glimpses of them since it fluttered too quickly and closed its wings whenever it sat down.

Presently it suspended itself upside down from one of the pea-blossoms and inserted its long tongue into a tiny hole at the base of the flower. The wings closed and showed black and white markings on a dove-grey background. As it sucked the honey, it was oblivious to my presence and I managed to get very near for some close-up pictures.

A second butterfly came to visit the same flower, and then a curious-looking bug also settled there. This turned out to be a sleek, velvety, grey creature with shimmering gold-coloured bands across its body and huge black eyes. It regarded me warily as it dipped its tongue into the sweetness of the pink flower. It certainly was happy hour at Hatta.

Wadi Halew

We had just traversed an extremely rocky wadi and climbed on to the bank at the far side. The road curved around a hill and suddenly a dozen boulders on the hillside seemed to come alive - partridges! Their protective colouring would have made them completely invisible to us if only they had sat still. But as they ran uphill, away from us, we could observe them quite easily. Still, because of their nondescript plumage, it was not possible to identify them properly. I have seen quite a few of them lately, groups of more than ten birds, in the hills alongside wadis. Are there more around at this time of the year, or am I becoming more observant?

The next part of the wadi which we had to cross still contained water. Huge clumps of reed (*Phragmites australis*) and bullrushes (*Typha domingensis*) grew between the rocks. When we stopped the car, the splash of the water on the stones intermingled with the song of many birds. We got out to investigate the area.

Several species of dragonflies and damsels flitted low over the pink algae that covered the pools. One settled down on a rock and I leaned close to get a better look. Its body was metallic red with a golden tinge, and the wings had orange splotches at the base and black spots at the tips. It looked spectacular against a background of silver sequins, created by the sunlight reflecting off the water. A small brown beetle rowed furiously upstream. A flock of silverbills whirled across the rockface of the adjacent hill like a sudden flurry of snowflakes. A Hume's Wheatear flashed its black and white feathers with a small cry of protest at our intrusion.

The rocky hillsides that formed the valley were riddled with caves, made for the greater part by erosion. One was clearly inhabited, probably by a fox, to judge by the lighter sand that marked its entrance.

I picked some bullrushes and when I dropped one it exploded into a cloud of plumed seeds that drifted away in the breeze like miniscule parachutes.

The large plumes of the reed grass caught the sunlight and looked like luminous pennants fluttering in the breeze.

Someone in our group cried out suddenly as he slipped on a wet rock and fell headlong into the stream. His light-coloured clothes were caked with pink and orange algae. We laughed at the idea of getting drenched in the three inches of water that a flowing river in a desert country consists of!

The fact was, however, that we could only continue our trip after the clothes had been washed and dried!

A spectacular red dragonfly.

Kalba

The long drive across the Hajar mountain range had been dusty and bumpy and the blue waters of the khor near Kalba looked enticingly cool. We sat down in the shade of the only tree on the near side of the inlet to have some refreshments.

The mangroves (*Avicennia marina*) on the far side grew thickly and behind the lush green of the marsh the mountains rose in range after range of blue-grey peaks. The little waves at our feet danced with joyous sparkles. A large bird skimmed across, heading out towards the sea.

We had been sitting quietly, when a small movement from one of us suddenly made the mud at our feet come alive. Dozens of crabs scampered into their holes, from which they had emerged so slowly that we had not noticed them before. As we sat motionless again, one after the other poked out its head with the prominent eyes, waving one large claw in front of them as if to test the air for safety. From a distance they looked grey like the mud, but when CC caught one, we looked at it closely and were surprised to find its carapace had shades of blue and purple, while parts of its claws were red.

Since we had a 4WD at our disposal, I wanted to investigate how far the inlet extended. We followed it around the first bend and were rewarded with the sight of a large flock of wading birds. The large Grey Herons were easy to identify and we counted half a dozen. The smaller Reef Herons occurred in even greater numbers and in both black and white plumage. One large bird was too far off to identify without field glasses and we had unfortunately forgotten to bring ours.

Where the spit of land between the khor and the sea narrowed, we parked the car and walked across the beach. Out in the blue waters of the strait, brown and red tankers lay high on the waves, waiting for safe passage to oil ports. The beach was a dull grey and stretched for miles northwards.

A large dark shape drew our attention and, when we approached it, it turned out to be the body of a Green Turtle (*Chelonia mydas*).

These sea turtles used to have a breeding colony on the coast, near Jebel Ali, in an area that is now completely built up. They swim great distances and are found in many seas all over the world. Unfortunately, they and their eggs are popular as gourmet delicacies and their numbers are rapidly dwindling.

Avicennia marina, the mangrove, forms a habitat for many birds.

This poor creature, whose cause of death we were unable to determine, had obviously made its very last trip to this coast.

We walked along the beach on the wide stretch of sand bordered by the new Kalba boulevard. A few barasti huts were festooned with rows of drying fish. A couple of reed boats lay close by. These are actually made from the centre ribs of palm leaves, bound together in bundles and shaped to form a hull. The method of tying these bundles together is identical to that used by ancient boat builders of the Euphrates and Tigris river areas and similar to the methods used in Egypt and on Lake Titicaca in Peru! Definite links between all these cultures have not been proved conclusively, but the coincidence of similar boatbuilding techniques in areas so far apart is intriguing.

The disadvantage of the palm leaf boats is that the more woody ribs have less floating capacity than the bundles made of reed. I have been told that the palm leaf boats will float for a maximum of four or five hours, after which they have to dry out again. Kalba fishermen must be fast workers or good swimmers- or both!

At the tideline there were hundreds of shells. The prettiest ones were the architectonica: circular, tiered structures, decorated with dots and dashes. A large variety of cowries in all sizes occurred and also ones that resemble bubbles abounded. Unfortunately, so did the tar-globules that soon blackened our feet and sandals.

One of us picked up a beautiful textile cone. The orange pattern was intricate, but part of the shell had broken off. Then someone else exclaimed with surprise: he had found an almost perfect skeleton of a trunk fish. This fish has an outer skeleton of hardened scales in addition to its backbone. In fact, the only movable part of the fish is its tail which it uses as rudder and oar simultaneously. I had seen these curious fish often while snorkeling. This skeleton was fascinating, as it showed the delicate lacework of its scales to perfection. Each scale was a six-times-perforated hexagonal structure and fitted with its neighbours like the cells of a honey comb.

The brightest colours on the beach were of the bi-valves. They ranged from salmon pink through bright orange to dark red, with their irregular shapes adding variety. A large piece of staghorn coral had a small brain coral growing between its branches; another piece of coral had been abraded by the action of water and sand to a smooth, wavy structure that looked like petrified surf. Later, I made an arrangement of corals and shells that serves well as a table decoration in this country where flowers are hard to come by.

skeleton of trunk fish p'85

Wadi Hail

There was quite a bit more water in Wadi Hail than the last time I had been there. It gurgled between the boulders to collect in small pools on which pond skaters were scratching their messages. The oleander bushes with their dark leaves and bright flowers contrasted vividly with the apple green of the sidr trees against the back-drop of palms - a lush environment and a feast for the eyes that are used to barren gravel plains and sandy hills.

A flash of colour flitted between the clumps of grass at the edge of a pool and when it settled down, it turned out to be a bright red-and-purple dragonfly with red eyes. Its lacy wings were spread out on either side of its body - and that is the characteristic by which a dragonfly can be distinguished from a damselfly. One of the latter landed just then on a twig nearby. It had a thin body and held its wings folded together above its back. It was powder-blue from tip to toe (if damselflies can be said to have toes). The wonderful colours of these insects never cease to amaze me: I have seen them in blue, purple, slate grey and metallic green and red.

CC squatted by a pool, feeling with his hand around the edge of the rocks. I started to say: "This is the pool where we saw the Giant Waterbug last time", when he exclaimed: "I think I have found a crayfish," and pulled back his hand - from which dangled the Giant Waterbug.

This six-inch ferocious-looking character is quite as aggressive as it looks. It has powerful front legs with which it grabs its victims (small frogs, beetles, etc.) and holds them while it sucks the life out of them.

The plant life along Wadi Hail is abundant and I saw three yellow-flowering plants that day. The small senna plant (*Cassia italica*), the seeds of which are used as a laxative; a large shrub, as yet unidentified by me, which had flowers growing in clusters like flaming torches; and a third four-inch diameter flower growing in abundance on lush bushes.

They looked similar to the *Tecoma stans* that is a

A fragile damselfly sits with folded wings.

The "dthub" track meanders from bush to bush.

cultivated garden shrub. Here it seemed indigenous, since many bushes could be seen all the way up to the top of the steep hill on either side of the wadi. It was later indentified as *Tecomella undulata,* and it is not known how it was introduced in the Emirates.

When we had to leave, I knew for sure that more exploration was necessary in future.

Tracking

After our visit to Bahrain in April when we first met the Spiny-tailed lizards (*Uromastix microlepis*) or dthub, we had resolved that we wanted to have a close look at them in the UAE, too. I had fallen in love with these relics of pre-historic times, gentle dragons of the desert. Because they are considered gourmet food, their number has dwindled. But I heard of a place where they had been sighted before, and so, on a cool Friday morning, we set out towards their reported habitat.

We drove towards Sweyhan past numerous farms, their lush green contrasting sharply with the orange dunes around them. We admired the stubborn courage with which trees, shrubs and grasses were grown in such adverse conditions. The colour of the sand dunes turned lighter and whiter as they leveled out. The road passed through the middle of a large salt flat covered with bizarre-looking aubergine-coloured saltbushes. We stopped and walked among them.

From one of the bushes a small creature lept at us. It was a hungry tick, which obviously mistook us for camels. It fell into the sand and immediately set course for my feet. When it reached me, I stepped aside, and without pausing the tiny thing changed course and made a beeline for my toes again. We repeated the game over and over and found out that, unless we moved more than six feet away, it always knew where to find us. For such a small arachnid, it had powerful sense of direction! We were almost sorry that we could not accommodate it!

After a long drive, we reached the home of the dthub. Unlike Bahrain, no lizards were easily seen, sunning themselves among the bushes. So we just started walking into the desert at random. Not ten yards from the road, we came across a dthub - track. We were not sure which way the lizard was heading, so we each followed its track in opposite directions, as it wound around zygophyllum bushes and stands of dry grass.

CC turned out to be going the right way, for he found the lizard's burrow. Its owner was nowhere in sight, unfortunately. Encouraged by our find, we started looking for more tracks, and we saw many different ones; little dung-beetle tracks, bird tracks, and tracks of smaller lizards. The latter could be followed easily, until they abruptly disappeared in an area of loose sand. It looked like the animal just "sank without a trace" there... and that is just what happened when we saw one. A large skink or Sand fish ran ahead of us and then disappeared under the surface. CC immediately dug into the sand, but we were unable to locate it again.

I found out what the tracks of a Desert hare look like when I disturbed one, which was resting in a small hollow in the sand. Its colour blended so well with its surroundings that I was upon it before I noticed it. It jumped away to sit a few yards away for a moment, its ears translucent pink in the sunshine, then it darted off across the dunes.

Among all the tracks we did not find another one of a Spiny-tailed lizard. No droppings, no burrows, not a sign of them anywhere. The reason for their absence was obvious. There was no food for them in this area any more. The goat and camel tracks that abounded were witness to the cause of this. All the shrubs, which were already stunted due to the drought, had been grazed to mere dots of vegetation.

One of these tiny clumps still sprouted a minute red pea-flower, by which I could recognize the plant as an *Indigofera intricata.* But no dthubs could stay alive here and we saluted the "last of the Mohicans" as we walked past its burrow on the way back.

I wished that a reservation could be created for these wonderful animals, before they disappear altogether. By the time people have realised that there *was* a heritage in the desert, it may well be too late.

The track of a Sand fish disappears abruptly where the reptile goes underground.

Madhaba

We had just turned on to a rougher track when I saw a movement to my left. A Kestrel Falcon swooped down to investigate a possible prey on the gravel plain. As he rolled and turned at my eye level. I could see the sunlight through his widespread light brown feathers - then he was gone, up into the vast blue sky.

When we were within a few hundred metres of

the mountain range we stopped. To the right was a large oasis which we judged to be very old from the size of the date palms. Beyond were the rugged Omani mountains. Just in front of us was a deep cleft in the mountainside where a wadi had cut through the sediments to form a canyon with several waterfalls.

The bank at the edge of the wadi was some 15 metres high, and from our vantage point we had a marvellous view of a string of crystal clear pools below us. Some were white with calcite deposits, others appeared poisonous yellow because of some yellow-green algae they contained, yet others were turquoise or emerald green, depending on their depth. A huge light blue dragonfly skimmed the surface of the pools. Close by a black and white bird settled on a rock - a Hooded Wheatear. It sat looking at us for quite a while, so that we could identify it easily by its pure white head, throat and belly. Lower down a different wheatear, with a black head, but a white throat and belly, flew across the water: a Hume's Wheatear. A couple of Rock Swallows were busy catching insects, swooping across the rockface.

We made our way down to the pools. It was curious that they seemed lifeless when you approached them, but, if you sat down for a while and waited, little fishes emerged from beneath overhanging rocks and clumps of algae. In most pools two different species were prevalent, a sleek black-and-silver one, and a slightly fatter type with a blunt head. In one pool this latter species had a red anal fin and a blue spot on its tail - or was this yet another species? And why did it only occur in that one particular pool?

Besides the fishes, there were damselfly larvae, two species of snails, backswimmers and an occasional leech to be found. One tiny pool - only about 20 cms across and almost dried up - contained a concentration of water-snails. It seemed likely that they would perish if the rains did not come soon. I proposed a rescue operation, but CC pointed out that creatures that had survived for so many ages in a desert environment would probably last without our help a little longer!

In one of the pools near the waterfall CC spotted something unusual. Two Water Scorpions were struggling in a close embrace. It looked as if one had attacked the other and was in the process of sucking the life out of its victim. CC picked up the bugs and tried to pull them apart. It was easy to see

the long appendage at their rear ends and we were surprised to find out that it consisted of two filaments. It did not look like a breathing apparatus, as is depicted in my encyclopedia.

Once separated, both victim and attacker seemed perfectly all right, so maybe this was not a predatory attack, but rather a romantic engagement that we had disturbed...

We waited for a bit to see whether the two would find each other again, but they hid beneath the rocks.

The valley narrowed and we had to climb across a rocky outcrop to reach the last bend before the waterfall. The late afternoon sun did not reach here any more, the cliffs on either side rose high and cast a deep shadow on the waterfall and the pool.

A narrow stream of water rushed down from a height of 10 metres or so into the black pool below, that was fringed with some grazed stands of reed and a few tephrosia bushes. A half dozen toads jumped away in front of our feet.

We debated climbing up the sheer cliffs to the top of the waterfall, but decided instead to retrace our steps and find an easier way up.

So we climbed up the steep bank again and skirted the plain, following a goat track which wound between the rocks and boulders towards the higher plateau. At one point we traversed a ridge, with steep drops on either side. To the left we could see the alluvial plain with some ripples of sand dunes in the distance. On the right the tall palms of the oasis were visible - a green garden overflowing the banks of the wadi. Far away, the rugged peaks of the Omani mountains rose dark blue against the lighter blue sky.

The plateau, when we reached it, was much larger than you would expect. It was empty except for a few acacias and some bright green zygophyllum bushes on the burnt sienna rocks. On the right the wadi meandered at the bottom of a canyon, which in some parts was more than 30 metres deep. It was impossible to get down to the water level at this point, but at the far end of the plain, we only had to slither down a scree slope to reach it.

We followed the course upstream until the wadibed ran dry. In several places there were springs - the water emerging from hidden aquafers at the contact points between the base rock and the layered sediments on top. Maidenhair ferns quivered above these tiny trickles and where pools had collected, reed grass and oleanders grew to impressive heights. Fishes and tadpoles were numerous and here and there a dragonfly added a touch of colour to the scene.

Once I spotted an agama, who regarded me with beady eyes and a froglike "smile" before it fled with a series of quick high jumps. I thought it was a curious way for a lizard to move.

On our way back we climbed down some rocky slopes to a deep green pool — a perfect place for a swim. In this sunny pool the water was refreshing. But when we followed the stream through a narrow gorge, the water - unheated by the sun's rays - was breathtakingly cold. Then we emerged into sunlight again. Gratefully, we climbed on to the warm rocks and sat down to take in the surroundings. The gorge had opened up into an oblong valley. At our feet the water fell 10 metres down into another pool, bordered with oleander and moringa trees. Rock Swallows and dragonflies went about their business and the afternoon sun roasted us gently. Life was perfect, except for that cold way back to the trail.

Heading for the car we walked through the dry wadibed. To our right the bank towered some 15 metres above our heads. The first three metres consisted of bedrock and on top of that lay countless layers of sedimented limestone. The bedrock was also layered in dark brown slabs with strips of white here and there. These layers, however were not horizontal, but nearly vertical.

We tried to figure out how this sheer wall was created. First, aeons ago, the bedrock was formed under immense pressures. Then, maybe at the time when the Arabian peninsula was still part of the African continent, the crust of the earth moved and folded and this part of the bedrock was uplifted to the 80° angle it was at now.

Heavy rains wore down the mountains and sheets of water flowed slower and slower across the wide plains of the peninsula, always depositing mud and slush, with small rocks - forming layer upon layer of soft sediments. How long must it have taken to deposit ten metres or more on top of the bedrock?

Then, something changed. Instead of depositing more sediment, the water began to wear down the sedimented layers, slowly carving a gully, a ditch, a channel and eventually a gorge and wide riverbed. How long did it take to wear down the layers of sediment and then, even slower, the bedrock to the level at which we were now standing? The climate

Bee on Schweinfurthia papillionacea.

The geological history can be read from the steep wadi banks.

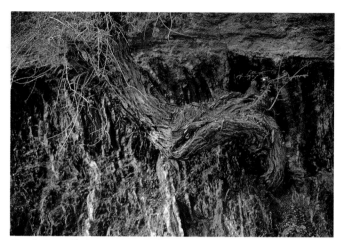

Gnarled trunk of an ancient ghaf tree.

must have been quite different. The rains must have been heavy and frequent, the land riddled with fast-flowing rivers which ran all the way down to the sea. Of course, the coast was much closer to the mountains then. The waters of the sea receded and the rivers became longer and shallower.

Then the sand that was created by the action of water and wind on the rocks, collected and eventually silted up the rivers. Now the wadis disappeared into the dunes, only to reappear as creeks along the far-off coastline.

I am not *sure* that it happened like this, but how else can the blind loops of the creeks of Dubai and the other coastal cities be explained? Are the courses of the rivers still traceable underneath the sand dunes? Could one, for instance, follow a line of ghaf trees from the end of Dubai creek to a wadi coming down from the Hajar mountains?

Clinging to the wadi bank, emerging from the lowest level of the sedimented limestone, was a grandfather of ghaf trees. The trunk was gnarled and twisted, measuring some 40 cms in diameter, and the crown rose up to the level of the plain above, the fine leaves drooping like a transparent green veil over the brown rocks. The bark of the tree was ridged and brittle, the grey brown colour matched the background of rock so closely that, but for the green leaves, we could have easily missed noticing it.

The seedling of this tree was here long before I was born. The years by which we measure the passage of time are so insignificant compared to the age of nature. And the disasters and joys that we experience in a year have no impact compared to the force that created this wadi and this

tree. Yet, we with our short life-span and our dull senses, are the only creatures who can consciously enjoy all this beauty, and ponder on the miracles that created it.

The Praying Mantis

December is not a good time for botanists. There was little of interest to see on the salty sands of Ayn Al Faydah. As a matter of habit I recorded all the plants I encountered: *Zygophyllum qatarense, Hammada elegans, Heliotropium kotschyi* and several salt-bushes. The *Limonium stocksii* shrubs that grow here were not in flower, but I knew the tamarix should be flowering. However, none of the tamarix trees that mingled with the numerous mesquite trees showed any colour. The reeds on my left were in full flower, and row upon row of graceful plumes swayed in the breeze, the sunlight lighting up the silky hairs against the black background of the Jebel Hafeet. The silence around me was profound; only my footsteps thudded softly on the crusty sand. Foxes or wild dogs had frequented this place - there was a little path outlined in the rain-splashed mud. I followed it and, lo and behold, it led me to what must be the only flowering tamarix in the area! I selected a few nice branches to photograph. The blossoms are pink and look like delicate bells. The fruits make a nice contrast, being bright red and triangular in shape. Both fruits and flowers occur at the same time.

As I fiddled around with my camera lenses, I made the first nice discovery of the day: a bizarre Praying Mantis. It had protuberances on its belly, a thorax with scalloped edges ending in spines, and fringes on the two front pairs of legs. Its head was adorned with two graceful antennae, that curved like a gazelle's horns. Its abdomen was curled upwards over its back - later CC told me that this is the case with *young* mantises. The huge eyes each had a small black dot, and these were aimed at me no matter where I positioned myself. The eyes seemed to roll in every possible direction, even backwards!

Apparently these dots are not pupils, but since they *look* like pupils, they do make you feel watched. The insect was striped in shades of beige, with here and there a white spot or a spine ending in black, with black claws and dark brown antennae. In spite of this striking appearance (or maybe because of it) it was almost undetectable against the background of pink and beige tamarix flowers. If it had not moved I would probably have taken it for a bunch of flowers. In fact, when I had my film developed, the mantis featured on one of the photos, hidden between the blooms!

When I retrieved my glasses from amidst the tamarix branches, where they had fallen, I discovered that the lenses were all sticky and fogged up. When I tried to clean them, it turned out they were covered with a salty liquid. I picked a twig and licked it. It was extremely salty to the taste. Even though I knew, in theory, that a salt-tolerant plant excretes salt, I had not realised this was the logical result — salt-crystals on the outer surface of the plant. Now, I'll never forget!

Midweek in Hatta

The rains that had drenched Dubai had not reached far inland. Hatta and Al Ain only had an hour-long shower which meant that the dirt-roads were still passable for my non-4WD-car.

As we carefully negotiated the vicious road-humps in Hatta village, I had ample time to point out the sights to my visitors. A flock of goats was being led by a beautiful, long-maned billy-goat, who strutted about with his goatee proudly sticking forward; Arabic coffee pot motifs on the brightly-painted iron doors; and a curly-haired kid staring at us from a safe distance.

Then we were among the multi-hued layered rocks that are so typical of the area. In the hollows between the hills evidence of the recent rains was visible as a sprinkling of green. Although it all looked like grass, I knew that many of the sprouting plants would probably be the tiny white lily *Asphodelus fistulosus.*

The gravel road billowed like an orange ribbon over the hills, descending steeply to cross wet wadi-beds, before climbing at awesome angles up to the next summit. At one point the road made a sort of dam across a wadi, and water had accumulated on one side to form a small lake. We stopped the car so that CC could investigate the pool. The silence of the hills was wonderful after the banging and rattling of the car. While CC observed some fish, that seemed to be a new species to him, my mother and I walked slowly up the road. A few metres off the road a large plant showed yellow...a new flower? But when I

came closer, it turned out to be a diseased plant with yellow leaves. Right next to it were two flowering plants, though: a *Salvia macilanta* with lavender labiate flowers protruding from hairy calyces, and a fine plant with narrow leaves and minute flowers and fruits that resembled those of *Euphorbia prostrata.* And, sure enough, when I picked a branch to add to the specimen collection, white milky sap exuded from the stem - as in all euphorbia.

But, on the whole, the rocks looked quite barren - shades of brown and ochre, with occasional rounded rocks of white magnesite.

Then I saw something that made my day. A little cloud of "pink smoke" was hanging between the rocks, almost too hazy to be real. I blinked, but it was still there. I had read about this. The Arabic name is "hadimdam" which supposedly means "pink smoke". The pink haze is in fact a fragile network of pink stems, as fine as hairs, and tiny pink flowers that tremble at the end of the 20 cms long stems. The plant named after a countryman of mine, is *Boerhavia elegans.* The leaves are dark green, oblong, and are grouped together near the ground. I had seen the plant with just a few stems and flowers many times before, but it needs a good-sized specimen before the effect of the "pink smoke" is created. This was a large plant - the leaf rosette being 35 cms in diameter and the pink cloud above it just about the same size.

When we returned to the hotel, CC spotted one of our favourite birds on the lawn. A Hoopoe was busy probing the soil for termites. It was a beautiful bird, pinkish brown with checkered black and white wings and a black tipped crest on its head. The black tail was banded with white. Most of the time the crest was lying flat, but from time to time, after a particularly satisfying morsel, the bird would look up and raise its crest, spreading it like a fan from back to front. I would have liked to hear the hoopoe call, after which it is named, but since this bird does not nest here, there is no chance of hearing it.

A young Praying mantis.

An anxious desert gecko.

A delicately constructed cocoon.

Swallow-tail butterfly on Lantana.

CC told us an interesting fact about the hoopoe. Whereas most birds, when they hatch, produce more or less firm packets of faeces that the parents can throw out of the nest, young hoopoes have liquid faeces, that is squirted around and makes the nest and its surroundings a noisome mess. Hence an old German saying: "You smell like a Hoopoe!"

As we walked back through the parking lot, we saw a swarm of butterflies around a lantana hedge. We approached quietly. There were several kinds of butterflies. The Painted Lady was present in great numbers. This is perhaps the most widespread butterfly in the world. The insects fluttered restlessly from flower to flower, landing only for split seconds. I wondered if it was possible for them to feed in so short a time. But maybe they were just smelling, sampling. Two butterflies were much larger: Swallow tails. They sat for long stretches of time on the flowers, their handsome yellow and black wings outspread. This is something one can only see in the cool days of winter here. For most of the time the temperature is too high, and the butterflies will keep their wings closed, to reduce the surface area and prevent dehydration. A third type of butterfly lay on the grass. It was dark blue, almost black, with barely visible markings. We thought it was dead and I wanted to have it - but just as I bent to pick it up, it flew off, only to settle a few feet away. It was also enjoying the gentle winter sunshine, so we left it undisturbed.

A New Year weekend

It was a clear day and the view across the orange dunes to the blue mountains beyond was superb. Among the roadside bushes were the broom-like *Leptodenia pyrotechnica* plants, back lit by the sun and sparkling with tiny stars - the velvety yellow flowers that are attached in clusters to their leafless branches.

Soon after leaving Al Ain we spotted a group of vultures some 20 yards from the road, sitting among the hammada bushes, obviously feeding off some carcass.

One was a common Egyptian Vulture, but the other two were much larger, with oddly wrinkled brown heads: Lappet-faced Vultures. As we watched from the car (always a good hide), they took wing and sailed across the plain - a wonderful sight, for these birds have become rare. It was good to know that there are still some around.

Near the Masafi roundabout I saw an area with trees that were also similar to broom in their appearance. We stopped and walked over to them, but they were not in flower. However, the large seed pods from last year might aid in identifying them. So I picked a few. (Later, the tree was identified as *Moringa peregrina,* proving the proverb: "By the fruit one shall know the tree").

CC walked through a conduit that passes underneath the road. A dwarf gecko was, for once, not fast enough to escape and ended up involuntarily posing for some pictures. It was smaller than CC's little finger and sat, gulping anxiously with bulging eyes, clinging to CC's thumb with its padded toes.

From the cement ceiling of the duct hung a strange structure: a series of square tubes that seemed to be built out of small pieces of straw - but where did the straw come from? Some tubes were closed with a whitish substance, and some were open and empty. They were obviously the cocoons of some insect.

We continued on our way and our next find was a fox, unfortunately fatally hit by a car. Since he was quite grey, we thought at first that it was the rare Ruppell's fox, but a closer look showed that it was just an ordinary red fox, of which there are many around.

As we neared the coast, we could see the pretty candles of the desert hyacinths emerging from the salty soil. It reminded me that one year was almost over, and another was beginning in which we could explore more, and maybe find some of the rarer plants and animals.

Dangers of the desert

The desert in our part of the world is not very hazardous. Of the plants, none are dangerous or harmful, although one could get diarrhoea from eating the fruits of the desert squash.

On all the many trips I have made in the last four years, I have encountered only a few potentially dangerous animals. And they have always fled rather than attacked.

I do not know if our largest reptile, the Desert Monitor, could inflict bad wounds if he were cornered. But why find out? Most animals are more

The Hoopoe is a common migrant visitor (photo: M West).

A sandracer is an elegant and fast-moving snake.

Sandboas are harmless and beautiful.

A Sandviper is poisonous and dangerous.

A Camel spider looks ferocious but does not have a poisonous bite.

interesting when observed from a distance while they go about their daily activities, than when they are brought into a state of fear and confusion.

The snake most often encountered on wadi bashes is the Wadi Racer - and unfortunately it is often killed for its supposedly dangerous bite. In fact, the snake is utterly harmless, unless you are a toad or a fish. Its cousin, the Sand Racer, is equally innocuous. Both snakes depend on speed rather than poison to protect themselves from harm.

Poisonous snakes *are* present, all belonging to the Viper family. The Sawscale or Carpet viper has a nasty bite, but can easily be avoided, because it makes a hissing sound to warn you off. But the Sand viper is potentially dangerous, because you can come upon it accidentally. It lies hidden in the sand, with just its eyes and nostrils showing and you could easily step on one. However, I believe that it will have felt the vibrations of your thudding feet as you approach and will disappear before this can happen.

It is more dangerous to lift stones or grope around in dark places with your bare hands. A scorpion can be disturbed and sting you. Of the two local species, the large black one looks more intimidating, but the smaller, pale-coloured scorpion has the stronger venom.

Bees and wasps can sting, too, but apart from the discomfort there is no danger, unless you are allergic to the venom, or have been stung by many.

Strangely enough, one of the most dangerous animals around is the tiny black ant that frequents many homes and gardens. It used not to occur here at all, but was introduced into the area when gardens and plantations were developed. It has a poison to which some people can be violently allergic. The most dangerous symptom is swelling of the mucous membranes of the throat, causing suffocation; or a

Of the two local scorpions the pale-coloured one is the more dangerous.

generalised effect, called "anaphylactic shock". It needs immediate professional treatment.

The ordinary insect stings can be treated with a mild anti-histamine, rubbed with vinegar, or (if you are in the desert and do not have any of these articles at hand) with urine. In case of a snake or scorpion bite: don't lose time by hunting and killing the animal. It is no longer dangerous and you do not need the dead snake to determine which anti venom needs to be given. Make sure the affected body part is moved as little as possible, is held as low as possible (beneath the level of the heart) and is kept as cool as possible. Then head for the nearest big hospital without delay (but driving carefully so as to avoid accidents). Tourniquets are advised **against** in general, since they cause more harm than they do good if applied by laymen.

I have not mentioned any of the dangers of the sea, of which there are many, since this is a book for landlubbers. But even they may come across a sea snake, washed up on the beach. Do not touch it - as dead as it may look, it could still be harmful and is best left alone.

These large ants are harmless, but the tiny black ones can cause a severe allergic reaction.

Most spiders are poisonous, but only to their prey-except for the Black widow spider (below) which can cause harm.

FIELD GUIDE

The guide section of this book consists of photographs of the more common wild plants of the UAE. They are grouped according to habitat — that is, the areas where they are most likely to be found:

C - for coastal area
S/G - for sand and gravel plains and hills
M - for mountains
P - for plantations
W - for wadis
GR - for grasses as a special section

Letters and numbers refer to entries in text.

Needless to say, one can find some plants in several habitats — nature has no strict boundaries. The photographs do not reflect the actual sizes of the plants and flowers. One needs to remember that most desert flowers are very small.

Prosopis juliflora (mesquite)   C1

Ipomoea biloba   C2

Halopeplis perfoliata   C3

Cornulaca leucacantha   C4

Salsola baryosma   C5

Sesuvium verrucosum   C6

Tamarix aucherana   C7

Zygophyllum hamiense   C8

Zygophyllum simplex (see also page 21)   C9

Launaea mucronata   C10

Pluchea ovalis   C11

Heliotropium kotschyi   C12

Sphaerocoma aucheri   C13

Limonium axillare   C14

83

Centaurea pseudosinaica   C15

Helianthemum lippii   C16

Plantago ciliaris   C17

Moltkiopsis ciliata   C18

Cistanche tubulosa (desert hyacinth)   C19

Cynomorium coccineum (red thumb see also page 7)   C20

Calligonum comosum (arta)   C21

Tribulus terrestris   C22

Leptadenia pyrotechnica   C23

Citrullus colocynthis (see also page 48)   C24

Dipterygium glaucum   C25

Rhanterium epapposum   C26

Tribulus omanense s.l. (R.Buckton)   C27

Hippocrepis bicontorta   C28

Neurada procumbens   C29

Erucaria hispanica   C30

Silene villosa C31

Senecio desfontanei C32

Eremobium aegyptiacum(see also cover and page 28) C33

Lotus halophilus C34

Prosopis cineraria (ghaf) S1

Cleome aff. glaucescens S2

Hammada elegans S3

Indigofera intricata S4

Convolvulus buschiricus S5

Euphorbia prostrata S6

Erodium laciniatum S7

Arnebia hispidissima (see also page 10) S8

Taverniera aegyptiaca S9

Crotalaria aegyptiaca S10

Cassia italica S11

Acacia tortilis (salam) G12

Aerva javanica   G 13

Rhazya stricta   G14

Fagonia indica   G15

Ochradenus baccatus (see also page 8)   G16

Jaubertia aucheri   G17

Argyolobum roseum   G18

Aizoon canariense (see also page 38)   G19

Anastatica hierochuntica   G20

Trichodesma ehrenbergii   G21

Zilla spinosa   G22

Scrophularia deserti   G23

Reseda aucheri   G24

Pergularia tomentosa   G25

Ochradenus aucheri   G26

Farsetia aegyptia   G27

Cuscuta planiflora   G28

Ephedra foliata (see also page 14)   G29

Diplotaxis harra (see also page 22)   G30

Savignya parviflora   G31

Anticharis glandulosa   G32

Moringa peregrina   M1

Astragalus fasciculifolius (see also page 25)   M2

Capparis cartilaginea   M3

Lavandula citriodora   M4

90

Lycium shawii   M5

Iphiona scabra   M6

Onychium divaricatum   M7

Caralluma europaea (Inset photo: D Livingstone)   M8

Ziziphus spina-christi (sidr)   P1

Heliotropium calcarium   P2

Launaea procumbens   P3

Lippia nodiflora   P4

Malva aegyptia   P5

Oxalis corniculata   P6

Adiantum capillus-veneris   P7

Solanum nigrum   P8

Portulaca oleracea   P9

Sonchus oleraceus   P10

Trigonella hamosa   P11

Withania somnifera   P12

Vernonia sp.   P13

Euphorbia hirta   P14

Chenopodium album   P15

Convolvulus arvensis   P16

Bacopa monnieri   P17

Alhagi maurorum   P18

Ricinus communis   P19

Sida urens   P20

Euphorbia peplus P21

Asphodelus fistulosus P22

Anagallis arvensis P23

Epipactis veratrifolia (see also page 66) P24

Rumex vesicarius (see also page 23) P25

Antirrhinum orontium P26

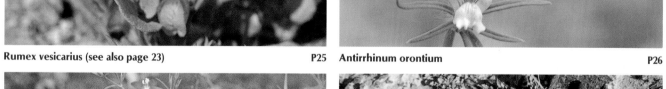

Centaurium pulchellum P27

Corchorus olitorius P28

Tephrosia apollinea   W1

Pulicaria glutinosa   W2

Nerium oleander   W3

Euphorbia larica   W4

Chrozophora oblongifolia   W5

Blepharis ciliaris   W6

Physorrhyncus chaemarapistum   W7

Salvadore persica   W8

Boerhavia elegans   W9

Boerhavia diffusa   W10

Capparis spinosa   W11

Forsskahlia tenacissima   W12

Cucumis prophetarum   W13

Dyerophytum indicum   W14

Cleome glaucescens   W15

Salvia macilanta   W16

Taverniera glabra   W17

Echinops sp   W18

Rhynchosia minima   W19

Pseudogaillonia hymenostephana   W20

Periploca aphylla   W21

Gypsophylla bellidifolia   W22

Leucas inflata   W23

Phragmites australis   W24

Chloris virgata GR1

Polypogon monspeliensis GR2

Pennisetum divisum GR3

Panicum turgidum GR4

Dactylocnemium aegyptium GR5

Aristida adscensionis GR6

Cymbopogon parkeri GR7

Stipagrostis plumosa GR8

GLOSSARY

astringent constipating

algae order of plant found in slow-moving or stagnant water

alluvial deposited by rivers or floods

antenna feeler of an insect

annual plant lasting only for one year

aphrodisiac exciting sexual desire

barchan sickle-shaped sand dune

bedrock early geological formation

biliary pertaining to bile or gallways

burrow hole in the ground dug by animal

calyx (pl. calyces) the outer covering or leaf-like envelope of a flower

camouflage method of visual deception

carapace the hard cover of the back of insects, tortoises, lobsters, etc

cathartic cleansing the bowels

composite belonging to the Compositae, the largest order of plants

corolla inner covering of a flower, composed of petals

crucifer belonging to the Cruciferae, an order of plants whose typical flower has four petals in the shape of a cross

entomology scientific study of insects

ephemeral lasting only for a very short time

falaj irrigation canal

feathered leaf composed of small leaflets opposing each other

germinate to begin to grow

ghaf desert tree: Prosopis spicigera

habitat the natural home of an animal or plant

herb plant with a soft stem which dies down after flowering

hygroscopic reacting to variations of humidity in the atmosphere

indigenous originating in the country

inflorescence arrangement of flowers on the main stem

labiate plant with flower formed in two parts, resembling lips

legume plant bearing seed pods with two valves

milkweed plant with milky sap

mollusc invertebrate animal with soft body and usually a hard outer shell

nakheel palm grove

parasite plant that lives at the expense of another, called its host

petal coloured flower leaf, part of the corolla

pistil seed-bearing, (female) organ of a flowering plant

pollination method of fertilisation of flowers

pore minute opening

predator animal that lives on prey

prostrate lying flat on the ground

rosette dense cluster of leaves resting on the ground

samr, salaam acacia tree

scalloped ornamental edge

sediment deposits laid down by water action

seedling young plant

sensory pertaining to the senses

sepal leaf-like part of outer covering of a flower, usually green or light brown in colour

serrated notched like a saw

sidr plantation tree: Zizyphus spina-christi

skink species of smooth-scaled lizard

specimen individual example

spray graceful branch with leaves and blossoms

stamen pollen-bearing (male) organ of a flowering plant

succulent full of juice

tonic medicine which tones up the system

trilobate with three lobes

umbel parasol-shaped flower-cluster

wadi river course

INDEX

Scientific names

Common names of plants

Al hammar	Arnebia hispidissima
Arabian primrose	Arnebia hispidissima
Arta	Calligonum comosum
Ayn al jamal	Anagallis arvensis
Blue pimpernel	Anagallis arvensis
Broombush	Leptadenia pyrotechnica
Bullrush	Typha domingensis
Camel's eye	Anagallis arvensis
Caper	Capparis cartilaginea
Desert hyacinth	Cistanche tubulosa
Desert thorn	Lycium shawii
Desert squash	Citrullus colocynthis
Eyelash plant	Blepharis ciliaris
Ferns	Onychium and Adiantum
Ghaf tree	Prosopis spicigera
Hadimdam	Boerhavia elegans
Hyacinth	Cistanche tubulosa
Incense grass	Cymbopogon parkeri
Indigo plant	Indigofera intricata
Jute plant	Corchorus olitorius
Khazamzam	Chloris virgata
Kurd	Ochradenus baccatus
Lavender	Lavandula citriodora
Lily	Asphodelus fistulosus
Maidenhair fern	Adiantum capillus-veneris
Mangrove	Avicennia marina
Mesquite	Prosopis cineraria
Muqaybil ash shams	Cleome aff. glaucescens
Oleander	Nerium oleander
Orchid	Epipactis veratrifolia
"Popcorn plant"	Pseudogaillonia hymenostephana
Ra'	Aerva javanica
Red thumb	Cynomorion coccineum
Reed	Phragmites australis
Salam	Acacia tortilis
Samr	Acacia sp.
Senna	Cassia italica
Sidr	Ziziphus spina-christi
Sodom apple	Calotropis procera
'Tha	Cornulaca leucacantha
Thistle	Echinops sp.
Toothbrush tree	Salvadore persica
"Velcro plant"	Forsskahlia tenacissima
Zahra	Tribulus deserti

Acknowledgements

My warm appreciation and grateful thanks go to the following people, without whom this book would not have come into being:

The founders of the Emirates Natural History Group, whose enthusiasm made it possible for so many people to get to know and appreciate the beauty of nature in the Emirates.

Rob Western, for helping me on my first hesitant steps into desert botany.

Loutfy Boulos, Professor of Botany at Kuwait University for his identification of my specimens and his continued interest and encouragement.

Claus C Mueller, zoologist at Al Ain Zoo, for sharing his extensive knowledge of wildlife and conservation with me.

Christian Gross, for providing his snake collection and wildcat for photography.

John Martin, for bringing me specimens and collating the index to this book.

The Khaleej Times for allowing use of the title from my weekly column and reprinting of material which first appeared in it.

And finally to

Shell

whose support made possible the publication of this book.

Marycke Jongbloed, Dubai 1987

The author

Flowers have been a life-long interest of Marycke Jongbloed as subjects for arrangements, photography and drawing, but she only took up botany after her first spring spent in the UAE in 1984.

Besides flowers, warm-blooded animals have always played a large part in her life; she has never been without one or more pets. The walks described in this book sparked a new interest: in insects and reptiles, as well as in the conservation of the wildlife of this area, large parts of which are threatened with extinction. It is her hope that this book may make readers more aware of both the beauty of desert nature and its precarious existence.

A graduate of Utrecht University and Rotterdam Medical Faculty, she has worked since 1970 in various fields of medicine in Holland, the USA, Indonesia and the UAE. After spending three years in Al Ain, she is now sharing a house in Dubai with varying numbers of marmosets, cats, fish, chickens and a cockatoo named Houdini.

THE ARABIAN HERITAGE SERIES

Arabian Profiles
edited by Ian Fairservice
and Chuck Grieve

Land of the Emirates
by Shirley Kay

Enchanting Oman
by Shirley Kay

Bahrain – Island Heritage
by Shirley Kay

Dubai – Gateway to the Gulf
edited by Ian Fairservice

Abu Dhabi – Garden City of the Gulf
by Peter Hellyer and Ian Fairservice

Fujairah – An Arabian Jewel
by Peter Hellyer

Portrait of Ras Al Khaimah
by Shirley Kay

Sharjah – Heritage and Progress
by Shirley Kay

Architectural Heritage of the Gulf
by Shirley Kay and Dariush Zandi

Emirates Archaeological Heritage
by Shirley Kay

Seafarers of the Gulf
by Shirley Kay

Gulf Landscapes
by Elizabeth Collas and Andrew Taylor

Birds of Southern Arabia
by Dave Robinson
and Adrian Chapman

Mammals of the Southern Gulf
by Christian Gross

The Living Desert
by Marycke Jongbloed

Seashells of Southern Arabia
by Donald and Eloise Bosch

The Living Seas
by Frances Dipper and Tony Woodward

Sketchbook Arabia
by Margaret Henderson

The Thesiger Collection
a catalogue of photographs
by Wilfred Thesiger

Thesiger's Return
by Peter Clark
with photographs by Wilfred Thesiger

Storm Command
by General Sir Peter de la Billière

This Strange Eventful History
by Edward Henderson

Juha – Last of the Errant Knights
by Mustapha Kamal,
translated by Jack Briggs

Fun in the Emirates
by Aisha Bowers
and Leslie P. Engelland

Mother Without a Mask
by Patricia Holton

Premier Editions

A Day Above Oman
by John Nowell

Forts of Oman
by Walter Dinteman

Land of the Emirates
by Shirley Kay

Enchanting Oman
by Shirley Kay

Abu Dhabi – Garden City of the Gulf
edited by Ian Fairservice
and Peter Hellyer

Arabian Heritage Guides

Snorkelling and Diving in Oman
by Rod Salm and Robert Baldwin

The Green Guide to the Emirates
by Marycke Jongbloed

Off-Road in the Emirates
by Dariush Zandi

Off-Road in Oman
by Heiner Klein
and Rebecca Brickson

Spoken Arabic – Step-by-Step
by John Kirkbright

Arabian Albums

Dubai – An Arabian Album
by Ronald Codrai

Abu Dhabi – An Arabian Album
by Ronald Codrai

MOTIVATE
PUBLISHING